D1596367

Discoveries & Considerations

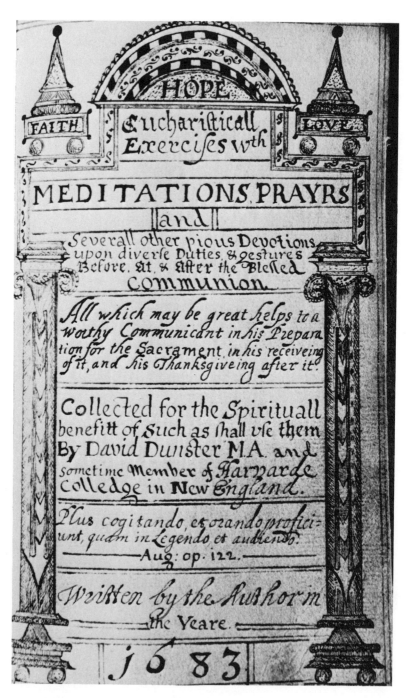

The 2d title page of David Dunster's *Gospelmanna*

DISCOVERIES & CONSIDERATIONS

Essays on Early American Literature & Aesthetics

Presented to Harold Jantz

Edited by
Calvin Israel

State University of New York Press
Albany, New York · 1976

Published with assistance
from the University Awards Committee
of the State University of New York
First published in 1976 by
State University of New York Press
99 Washington Avenue, Albany, New York 12210
© 1976 State University of New York
All rights reserved

Printed in the United States of America

Library of Congress Cataloging in Publication Data
Main entry under title:
Discoveries and considerations.
    CONTENTS: Jantz, H. American baroque.—Meserole,
H. T. New voices from seventeenth-century America.—
Arner, R.D. The structure of Anne Bradstreet's Tenth
Muse. [etc.]
    1. American literature—History and criticism—
Addresses, essays, lectures.   2. Aesthetics, American—
Addresses, essays, lectures.   3. Jantz, Harold Stein,
1907–   I. Jantz, Harold Stein, 1907–   II. Israel,
Calvin.
PS121.D55   810'.9   76-5424
ISBN 0-87395-340-1
ISBN 0-87395-341-X microfiche.

CONTENTS

INTRODUCTION

The confluence of voices of younger and older scholars in this book testifies to the rapid growth and development of early American studies in the last three decades, a growth and development prompted in a major sense by the publication of Harold Jantz's *The First Century of New England Verse* (1943). All of the writers represented here can attest to the importance of Professor Jantz's suggestions: that much more remained to be discovered, read, considered and evaluated in early American writings, and that until such time as scholars accomplished that research it was entirely defensible to set aside all evaluations of early American literature as unwarranted conclusions.

The first two decades (1943–64) were years of growing appreciation by early American scholars and students of the splendid guidance of Harold Jantz's criticism and bibliographies in *The First Century of New England Verse*. The period can be said to have ended with a meeting of early Americanists at the Modern Language Association convention in Chicago, December 1965. From that meeting, co-chaired by Professors Harrison T. Meserole and Brom Weber, with this editor as secretary and with Harold Jantz present, came the determination to maintain friendly and scholarly contact. That association formalized by two subsequent events: the founding of the journal *Early American Literature*, and the formation of an early American literature group within MLA. The growth of early American studies since can be seen in the large number of doctorates proposed and completed yearly and the thickness of the annual early American bibliographies in *PMLA* and *American Literary Scholarship*.

The contributions to this book were collected to honor Harold Jantz and to mark the first conference on Problems of Aesthetics in Early American Literature which was held 22–23 October 1971, under the direction of the Department of English, State University of New York College of Arts and Science at Geneseo. The conference was dedicated to Harold Jantz, and three of the papers read and rewritten for publication appear in this volume: Harold Jantz's keynote address on American early poetry, Harrison T. Meserole's discovery of David Dunster's seventeenth-century manuscript, and Julian Mates' examination of early theatre in America. These three essays, together with the other new articles written for this book, are dedicated as a festschrift to Harold Jantz.

The papers collected here are unified, in the main, by how significantly each discovery or consideration enhances the field of early American literature. That field is here extended in many directions, as the diverse approaches and methodologies of these investigations indicate. Among other matters, the papers focus upon early American poetry, aesthetics, intellectual history, biography, and literary history.

The first four papers are a coherent unit on seventeenth-century American Puritan poetry, beginning with Harold Jantz's "American Baroque: Three Representative Poets." The warmth of Professor Jantz is present in this paper as he recounts not only the difficulties encountered but also the joys and rewards of his long labor in the field of early American literature. He traces and defines the provocative term *baroque* as he applies it to early American poetry, and discusses, in the light of that definition, the artistry of three early American poets: Edward Johnson, John Fiske, and Edward Taylor.

The second paper is Harrison T. Meserole's "New Voices from Seventeenth-Century America," which announces the discovery of a new and significant seventeenth-century American poet, David Dunster. The field of early American literature is especially enriched and extended by the discovery of this talented poet, for the quality of Dunster's artistry, as Meserole suggests, elicits comparison with the major early American poet, Edward Taylor.

Two other papers on early American poetry close the first section of the book, and in these papers differing critical approaches to early American poetry may be observed. Robert D. Arner's paper, "The Structure of Anne Bradstreet's *Tenth Muse*," is an innovative approach to the longer poems of Anne Bradstreet. Bradstreet's long, "awkward" poems have always been less admired and treated with much less attention than scholars give her "charming" shorter ones, and it is the shorter ones, for this reason, which are most frequently anthologized. Arner discusses the aesthetic value of these longer poems and makes a clear place for them in the Bradstreet canon on aesthetic grounds. Bradstreet's artistic efforts to produce a unified book of poems are also discussed by Professor Arner, and his consideration of this facet of Bradstreet's talents enlarges our appreciation of her work. A contrast to Arner's methodology in criticism of early American poetry is evident in the more familiar approach by Thomas M. Davis and Arthur Forstater in their paper, "Edward Taylor's 'A Fig for thee OH! Death.'" Their paper concentrates upon a single Taylor poem rather than larger forms as they examine how Taylor worked his source materials into his poem. The Davis-Forstater article supports Taylor's sound reputation and reveals details about his conscious and unconscious artistry.

In the second section of these essays we find varying methodological approaches to early American literature and aesthetics: the relations between painting and culture; the relations between popular culture and theatre; the relations among history, politics, aesthetics, and theology; and the tracing of a singular literary figure-motif. Although these papers may be re-ordered to be read historically from seventeenth-century concerns to the present, the order in which they are offered should prove satisfactory.

The first is Roger B. Stein's investigation of the quality of American aesthetics in the years of the early republic. Concentrating upon the career of John Singleton Copley and his painting, *Watson and the Shark*, Stein explores for us the complex problem of understanding American aesthetic thought and practice in the nation's formative years. He interweaves formalist concerns with study of sources and influences, American and European, and a sense of the tradition of American seascape, in order to arrive at a sense of the aesthetic choices open to the American artist in the 1770s. Professor Stein further discusses how seascape in the American imagination can help us to understand the aesthetic meanings of the early American writer and artist, and suggests some ways in which that seascape looks ahead to the literary canvases of writers like Cooper, Poe, and Melville.

From painting we move to early American theatre in Julian Mates' "Theatre vs. Drama: Popular Entertainment in Early America." Professor Mates' paper explores the history of the early American stage as a form of cultural expression, clarifying the ways in which European theatrical forms were adapted to native purposes, and sometimes transformed and given new shape in comic opera, melodrama, and the minstrel show.

In taking up the challenge of Harold Jantz's statement about the importance of Edward Johnson's *The Wonder-Working Providence of Sion's Saviour in New England* as an early American work of art, Cecilia Tichi discusses Johnson's aesthetic concerns in her paper, "Edward Johnson and the Puritan Territorial Imperative." The Utopian motif, the apocalyptic vision, the "errand" to reconstruct the "wilderness," and other metaphors are not, she makes clear, uncommon in Puritan art and thought; these also underlie Edward Johnson's artistry. Professor Tichi systematically demonstrates that *Wonder-Working Providence* is a sustained metaphor, and that it must be understood in the framework within which the American Puritans operated: taking their interpretation of their "errand" from Genesis, they came to the New World to reconstruct it into an earthly paradise. As Tichi interweaves history, politics, aesthetics and theology in dealing with Johnson's work, she effects a transformation of conventional attitudes about American Puritan art and aesthetics.

The volume of essays is completed by Robert J. Gangewere's "Thomas Morton: Character and Symbol in a Minor American Epic." In this most delightful yet scholarly paper, Mr. Gangewere traces the figure—the image—of Thomas Morton in American literature as a motif from the seventeenth century to the present. As we learn, the symbol of Merry Mount also approaches epic significance in our literature, occurring as it does in the writings of Thomas Morton himself, William Bradford, Nathaniel Hawthorne, John Lothrop Motley, Charles Francis Adams, many modern novelists, and the modern poet Robert Lowell. This last paper, the tracing of a continuing literary motif—Thomas Morton of Merry Mount—is a cordial capstone to the volume.

It has been my pleasure and privilege to be responsible as editor for the revelation of these discoveries and considerations, and to announce them here in honor of Harold Jantz. Professor Jantz's extensive contributions to the field of German thought and literature (including the impact of those fields upon American letters) were honored upon the occasion of his sixty-fifth birthday, 26 August 1972, with the presentation to him of a volume of studies in those fields (*Traditions*

and Transitions: Studies in Honor of Harold Jantz, edited by
L. E. Kurth, W. H. McLain, and Holger Homann [Delp,
1972]). However, the many who know Professor Jantz's ac-
complishments in early American studies feel strongly that
American literature shares an equal place in his affections.
Harrison T. Meserole's words upon another occasion, the elec-
tion of Harold Jantz as an Honored Scholar of Early American
Literature, seem appropriate here:

> Professor Harold Stein Jantz created the field of American
> poetry as a separate area of study with the publication of his
> *The First Century of New England Verse* in 1943. It is still the
> standard bibliography of American puritan poetry, still a valu-
> able anthology of previously unknown poems, and will always
> remain an indispensable critical survey. It has already supplied,
> and will continue to do so, the basic material for numerous arti-
> cles and books. . . . We particularly esteem Professor Jantz's
> solid scholarship, his genuine originality, and the suggestiveness
> of his criticism and interpretations. . . . And, happily, there are
> more to come. We may shortly expect a new and completely
> revised edition of his *First Century of New England Verse,* and
> essays on the seventeenth-century American alchemist Eirenaeus
> Philalethes, on John Winthrop of Connecticut, and on Francis
> Daniel Pastorious. . . .

We present, then, this book of essays to Harold Jantz.

My deepest thanks go to the scholars who provided these
papers, and for their friendship and patience. I thank also the
Research Foundation of the State University of New York for
making both the conference on early American literature
(1971) and this book possible.

CALVIN ISRAEL
PIFFARD, N.Y.

I.

AMERICAN BAROQUE:

THREE REPRESENTATIVE POETS

Years ago, during a long visit in Spain, I went walking one sunny January morning through the streets of Seville. I stopped to ask a question, and something happened that has haunted me ever since, to the point of becoming almost symbolic or parabolic.

As I walked along I stopped at the window of a second-hand shop and among the junk I saw two or three good things that were worth asking about. So I went in and talked to the proprietor who, seeing my interest, took me through into a back room, also filled with second-hand odds and ends but with a better and larger sprinkling of antiques. After I had gone just to those pieces and examined them, he took me to a further room where the antiques were already more numerous and of higher quality, even with some paintings worth a second glance. Apparently here too I concentrated on just the right things, for he took me on to two further progressively better rooms, and when I passed the test here also, he opened up the back door to the last room, and I found myself in the hall of a magnificent palace. As we ascended the great stairway, I glanced over at my host and somehow he no longer looked like the second-hand dealer whom I had met just off the street.

As we went on from room to room and he talked to me about the fine paintings and splendid furnishings, I knew I was in the presence of one of the great antiquarians of Seville and that a strange piece of luck had befallen me.

The notion of a parable came years later when, on thinking over two quite different pieces of research, I saw that they had a sequence of features in common. There was an early first incident that aroused my attention but did not seem to promise much. This, however, led on to another insight or finding of greater worth or promise, and so on progressively until undreamed of new vistas opened up before me.

As for the early poetry, my original search was for something quite different: the unexpectedly important German antecedents of colonial New England intellectual history. This search took me to the greater and lesser libraries and historical societies, and as I went through dozens and hundreds of early colonial manuscripts and prints, various poems and sets of verses would turn up that were unknown to all the extant surveys and bibliographies of early American literature. Most of these verses were inconsiderable as art, though they were often interesting historically, and they did afford new insights into the temper and attitude of early colonial life. As time went on and the quantity of the new verse increased, a modest portion of quality also emerged. The first thrill came one late morning in Boston with the finding of the manuscript of Thomas Tillam's "Uppon the first sight of New-England June 29 1638." This is an authentic work of art.

At this point I must make a careful critical discrimination: an authentic work of art does not necessarily have to be one of the great masterpieces of world literature. On the other hand, one of the impressive works of world literature, even one that has gained for its author the Nobel Prize, may, a generation later, turn out not to be an authentic work of art.

The Tillam poem was the first of my new findings to win general acceptance. Louis Untermeyer saw its value though he never acknowledged its source, and from his time onward it has become a standard entry in the anthologies of American poetry.

Quite the opposite fate awaited the extensive manuscript of a dozen shorter and longer poems that turned up in Providence, Rhode Island. After my first laborious transcription of the nearly illegible handwriting I concluded that this verse was really as bad as all Puritan verse is supposed to be. But some inner voice warned me that I had better take another, closer look. When I did, and then a third, a fourth, and a fifth look, I found that I was facing a totally new and unexpected verse technique, without any known precedent, and this two centuries before Walt Whitman. When I found another different but equally original poet, I felt finally that it was worth doing a full-length study of the whole matter. After all, Thomas H. Johnson had previously discovered an early New England poet of unexpected quality, and now it appeared that there were others of true quality and notable orginality.

And so my survey of the first century of New England verse appeared, during the war, without benefit of final proofreading and with an assortment of printing errors added to my manuscript errors. But the reviewers were generally charitable and paid more attention to the new findings and insights than to the flaws inevitable in a pioneer work. With all that, a strange silence grew up around the book. There were incidental mentions here and there, but in the general surveys and discussions it seemed as though it had never been issued. All this changed a decade or so ago, suddenly and inexplicably. All at once there was a large group of young people busy in the field and some of them were fast becoming experts, adding materially to our knowledge and insight. They began to send me additions and corrections that were important supplements to the ones I had made during the intervening years.

At first it was a bit difficult to adjust to the new circumstances: in my early years I had written a pioneer work that

had, to be sure, met with a friendly reception, but had en-
gendered so slight an echo that I had virtually forgotten it
and turned to other things. All at once, there it was again, and
furthermore I found myself under the obligation of preparing
a new edition for which material had been accumulating from
the day it had been published.

On one point one critic continued to object to the book. He
looked with disfavor upon the word *baroque* and my use of
it to characterize certain aspects of the first century of American literature. This was inevitable, even though Austin Warren
had preceded me in this use, for the nineteenth century had
erected a solid wall of prejudice to protect us from the
baroque. In the field of art, to be sure, the wall was largely
demolished a half century and more ago, but in the field of
literature large sections of it remained standing till fairly recently, especially in the English-speaking world, despite the
early efforts of Sacheverell Sitwell and others. Only after the
term came to be accepted in France and even to be applied to
the great works of its golden age, did the English finally, hesi-
tatingly, and sparingly come to use it for their own Stuart
exuberance.

For American literature the term has hardly even been con-
troversial—it has barely continued to exist in a few subsequent
studies. However, the spirit in certain early American works
has long been recognized, and abominated. To Moses Coit
Tyler in 1878 Nicolas Noyes was the exemplar of all that was
wrong with the early verse; Tyler called him "the most gifted
and brilliant master ever produced in America, of the most
execrable form of poetry to which the English language was
ever degraded." Another verdict of this critic against Noyes
should, however, give us pause: "even in old age, he continued
to write the sort of poetry that, in his youth, had been the
fashion, both in England and America,— the degenerate
euphuism of Donne, of Wither, of Quarles, of George Herbert.
To this appalling type of poetry, Nicholas Noyes faithfully

adhered, even to the end of his days, unseduced by the rhythmical heresies, the classic innovations, of John Dryden and Alexander Pope." Now nearly a century later there are perhaps few people left who would care to maintain that John Donne or George Herbert are utterly beyond the poetic pale, or that Dryden and Pope have been an unmixed blessing to English poetry, rendering their predecessors forever unpalatable to refined poetic taste. And yet these old Victorian standards are still maintained in the criticism of early American literature, and the verdict on Noyes has been quoted with approval in our time.

Ironically, Noyes was not the most gifted and brilliant master of this style; Edward Taylor far outdid him in every feature here held up to scorn. His lyric cycle, "Gods Determinations," would have elicited pained shock from the very first page, where he exalts the Creator,

> Whose Might Almighty can by half a looks
> Root up the rocks and rock the hills by th'roots.

The genteel critic would probably have stopped in outrage before he came to "Christs Reply" to the Soul, with its yelping dogs, frightened chicks, kissing poles and meeting parallels. And the delightful final lyric where the saints ride to heaven in Christ's coach would have seemed a tasteless puerility to him. If Taylor escaped Tyler's damnation, it was only because he was safely tucked away in unread manuscripts until the era of prejudice was past and a man with the new tastes and judgments brought him to light.

With all that, Moses Coit Tyler has served us well: he has provided us with our first definition of American Baroque, however cross-grained, and, more subtly, he has stated a basic premise that is still widely accepted even though it is about as questionable as his views on the baroque. The assumption I question is that of a colonial dependence and cultural lag of seventeenth-century New England literature. Massachusetts and Connecticut were different: they started out as experimental stations, as "pilot plants" for the Puritan revolution. When Cromwell came to power, he invited a number of New Englanders back, and some did return, to positions of experienced leadership in the new Commonwealth. New England in several important respects was in advance of old England.

In literature one should probably speak neither of lag nor of leadership. It is better to speak of independence. American literature was to an unusual degree independent during its first hundred years. Only after the 1720s or '30s does it become a more fully dependent, a genuinely colonial literature, imitating the approved homeland models of Dryden and Pope in verse, of Addison and Steele in prose, though even in the eighteenth century there are some remarkable exceptions and deliberate deviations. The New England poets did know Dryden from the 1680s and '90s, but the best of them continued to go their own way and to develop their own sometimes highly original forms. We shall see this in several minor instances before we go on to the three greater poets. But first we should try to do better by the term *baroque*, which despite its dubious origins has gained entrance into the critical world.

Baroque is, of course, a character in art history, a somewhat disreputable though grand lady who was first given respectability by the great Heinrich Wölfflin. If she had remained confined to the the reasonably generous bounds of his categories and definitions, she would have remained an esteemed and useful member of learned society. But the original sin of her extravagant nature soon set her to roaming, back into the Counter-Reformation, into the late Renaissance, even though Wölfflin had tried to teach her how truly different she was from the superficially similar Mannerism of the late sixteenth century. She even vagabonded back into the more exuberant phases of earlier Renaissance and late Gothic, and before anyone could stop her, she was on familiar terms with Laocoön and other Hellenistic statuary.

Let us for today try to bring the baroque back to its own time and place in the seventeenth and early eighteenth centuries, where it stands for an intricacy, a richness, and a fullness that is always under masterful control, that can soar forth in a wide parabola from a specific instance, to encompass all relevant instances and, returning to its point of departure, thereby transmute it from a particular to a universal. It differs from the Mannerism that preceded it in the later sixteenth century by virtue of its continuity, its feeling for the whole that subordinates all the individual parts into an integrated unity, an inextricably interrelated complex of forces, with vast suggestive power beyond its statement, to be comprehended only by the active and creative reader. Its difference from the classicism that follows can perhaps be best expressed as a contrast to the definition of classical art that is generally attributed to Winckelmann, but goes back to his teacher Oeser and further back to Donner. These men of the early and mid-eighteenth century saw in classical art "a noble simplicity and a quiet grandeur," "edle Einfalt und stille Grösse." By contrast, we might define the baroque as "a noble complexity and an emphatic grandeur."

Now we face our real difficulty. How can we possibly imagine that American literature of the seventeenth century can live up to such a definition? It cannot, of course. Literature in all ages goes its usual pedestrian way, accessible to most, communicating to most, decorated with some of the colors of its times and trends, a few stylistic peculiarities that help to date it. Yet there are always the few poets who have a more intense vision of the essence of their times and who try to express it in a more concentrated manner. In New England there is no single poet who does this completely (there rarely is anywhere), but there are three who together do fulfill the demands and solve the problems of American Baroque. Edward Johnson does so in poetic rhythm and diction, John Fiske in poetic form and contextuality, Edward Taylor in poetic imagery and lyric ductility. Johnson masters the perspectives, Fiske the composition, Taylor the expression. Johnson has the epic scope, Fiske the contrapuntal unity, Taylor the transcendental relevance of the baroque. This does not mean that each is fragmentary. Each is complete in himself and a true poet. When we put them together, however, the full scope and possibility of American Baroque become visible.

Theirs was not a development in isolation. They had predecessors and contemporaries who in their more modest ways show whence they came and how they belonged to their times. Part of their strength came from the fact that the classical, the medieval, and the Renaissance traditions were not broken but remained alive in the continuum. It may seem a mere anachronism that a merchant from Bristol, Anthony Somerby, continued to write verse in the 1640s that made systematic use of the principle of Anglo-Saxon alliteration. But we can see that this medieval poetic technique was still alive and effective on a higher literary level even decades later in the brief poem by John Josselyn on a storm at sea. Renaissance Mannerism (in transition to early baroque) also survives in at least one specimen, old Nathaniel Ward's commendatory verses on Anne Bradstreet, with their tightly packed form, broken line, and telescoped imagery, so different from the equally rich but more generously disposed images and freely flowing forms of the full baroque. In the case of the strongest of the self-educated versifiers, such as Philip Walker, it would be difficult to distinguish between true independence of expression and sheer cussedness. By contrast, a sheep farmer, Samuel Bailey, shows a poetic control and satiric wit in his one known poem that is anything but unsophisticated.

As remarkable as it is brief is Joshua Moody's venture into free verse in a beautifully rhythmic balance of brief lines progressing by contrast and continuity. The poem shows how one tradition in free verse has its origins in the Roman monumental inscription or rather in the Renaissance continuation of it.

In subject surely the most unusual American poet of the
baroque was George Starkey, not so much for his royalist
political verse as for his versified *Marrow of Alchemy* (London, 1654–55). It was the first American poem to be translated
into another language and to be internationally circulated. In
a few passages it rises to real eloquence, and on the whole one
can say that if baroque man insisted on rhyme rather than
reason in his alchemy, no one in the seventeenth century did
any better than George Starkey. And yet, in one literary feature the poem is not to be underestimated: it released upon
the world one of the first of the American legends, a legend
that continues to haunt the imagination and to challenge the
intellect to penetrate its mysteries—so far without success,
even though no less a man than Kittredge bent his mind to the
task. It is the legend of the mysterious American adept,
Eirenaeus Philalethes Cosmopolita, on whom I have found
seventeenth-century reports from Denmark, Germany, Aus-
tria, Italy, and France, with two men of note claiming that
they knew him personally but were under a pledge not to
reveal his real name. The recent attempts to identify him with
John Winthrop the Younger of Connecticut are clearly refuted
by a letter from Winthrop himself, a letter that the recent
writers on the question have overlooked even though it is
easily available.

Perhaps best among the minor poets of pronounced originality was Richard Steere, especially for his powerful descriptive
poem, "On a Sea-Storm nigh the Coast." Its power is that of a
direct evocation of nature, without a trace of moral reflection
or subjective involvement, a pure impression of phenomena,
divinely objective.

For all his originality in this one poem and in a few passages
of others, Steere is, on the whole, a lesser poet, of good quality,
easy and pleasant to read. Eminently readable also and full of
surprises is Benjamin Tompson, though one has the feeling
that his startling spurts of originality are less the result of a

strong genius than of a volatile temperament and wild wit. At this time, as always, it was possible to be a good poet and yet remain conventional without marked originality. There was Roger Williams with his simple, distinguished, thoughtful poems on Indians and Christians. There was Anne Bradstreet who several times in her intimate familial poems attained a warmth and beauty of human sentiment that still has the power to move us. There was John Saffin, able in lyric and philosophical poem; the long popular Michael Wigglesworth; the Horatian Benjamin Lynde; and the student John Crowne, who wrote a novel with charming lyrics before he went to England to become one of the well-known Restoration dramatists and to have Henry Purcell set some of his poems to music.

Good as they were, we do enter a realm of greater dimensions when we come to the work of Edward Johnson (1598–1672). His *History of New-England*, generally called the *Wonder-Working Providence of Sions Saviour in New-England* (1653), does contain some 67 sets of verses, most of them mediocre to poor, a few showing flashes of poetic mastery. The best of them, variously anthologized, is not by him but by an earlier English poet, except in its poorer continuing stanzas. The picture changes when we turn from his verse to his ostensible prose. Moses Coit Tyler turned purple at the prose, but we had best put aside this critic entirely, since he allowed his outraged prejudice to involve him in errors of fact as well as of judgment. The reader who can approach Johnson's work directly and dispassionately will probably soon be impressed by his mastery of style and composition, and especially by his sure sense of what constitutes the truly epic, namely the elevation of a set of local events into the universal under the span of a great unifying vision. Johnson succeeded where most of the epic poets in and after the Renaissance failed: whereas they merely took over the conventional trappings of the epic, he had the sure feeling of the

artist for the essential behind the convention and found his
own valid and appropriate form for embodying this essence.
Not that the whole work is on such a level. Far from it. But
there is enough to show forth his epic mastery.

Most remarkable perhaps is the fact that he made a successful transfer of Homeric dactylic rhythms into English, a feat
that will appear all the more remarkable if we consider the
feeble and clumsy attempts to do so in England before his time
and the failure to do anything comparable for two centuries
after his time. The very first lines, a splendid proem, show his
epic scope and vision—

> When England began to decline in religion, like luke-warm
>   Laodicea
> . . . . . .

—But I have quoted this passage on an earlier occasion as well
as the fine narrative passage on the comet and Indian plague of
the two years before the first settlers arrived. Two other
briefer quotations will serve to illustrate, the first the beginning of that powerful hortatory section summoning all the
settlers to the service of this vision of a new commonwealth
on a new soil that is to be the prelude and model for the
reformation of the whole wide world (XV):

> And now all you whose affections are taken with wonderful
>   matters:
>   Attend!
> And you that think Christ hath forgotten his poor despised
>   people:
>   Behold!

Then there is the somewhat more irregular later passage on
the Lord's summoning the men fit to guide the new commonwealth (XLV):

> See here the Wonder-working Providence of Sions Saviour
>   appears

Much in gathering together stones to build up the walls of
    Jerusalem
(That his Sion may be surrounded with Bulworkes and
    Towres).
With a whispering word in the eares of his servants, he
    crosses
Then Angles of England from Cornewall to Kent, from
    Dover to Barwick. . . .

Such passages are an offense to the genteel critic and an
absurdity to the materialist historian. What we have in Johnson is the first panoramic prospect of the future of America
as the light and guide of the nations of the world, and also a
view of the deeply spiritual forces that propelled these few
coastal settlers and their followers through space and time and
generations across a continent and on to a new nation. The
work presents with the utmost candor the motivating forces
and the psychological impulses that led to the founding of
New England (and eventually of the United States), giving
just place to the transcendental, apocalyptic, millenarian,
utopian tendencies that were so strong in many of the leaders.
Modern historians, embarrassed at these phenomena and not
knowing quite what to do with them, have generally passed
over them in silence or discredited them, much to the falsifica-
tion of American history.

However, we too should be unfair to the work if we did
not note that Johnson, with all his high seriousness, had a
charming sense of humor and knew how to enliven his narrative with many a salty dash of satire and a vigorous human
realism. All these elements of humor, realism, narrative talent,
broad vision, fervid ideals, and epic power, though in different
proportion, are to be found in an earlier anonymous work that
I have attributed to Edward Johnson. It is the *Good news
from New-England* of 1648, regularly confused with Edward
Winslow's earlier work of the same title, and consistently

neglected. It is one of the most readable and enjoyable verse narratives of seventeenth-century America, full of humor, satire, exciting narration and vivid description, all of it held together by the force of a great vision and a high purpose. Johnson's last known poem, on Lake Winnepesaukee, is probably his most beautiful.

Variously in the *History*, especially in chapters XXIV and XXVI, there are what clearly seem to be allusions to or paraphrases of the first popular ballad of New England, one that was passed down by word of mouth and not transcribed and printed till the mid-eighteenth century. It was later called "Our Forefathers' Song," but is perhaps better called by its first three words, "New England's Annoyances." On grounds of style, content, and point of view it seems likely that Edward Johnson was the author. My first reconstruction and the first publication of the entire ballad appeared in Harrison T. Meserole's anthology, *Seventeenth-Century American Poetry* (1968). Since then further discovery and critical analysis of extant versions, and a crucial emendation, ventured by me, have carried the reconstruction farther toward completion, we hope.

Ten years younger than Johnson and worlds different from him was John Fiske (1608–1677), an esteemed pastor, physician, and school-teacher, but unknown as a poet until his verse was deciphered from one of the most difficult manuscripts of a century of bad handwriting. Of my first negative reactions I have already spoken; the verse seemed dry, harsh, and gnarled, with little grace and no music. Gradually it became clear that this judgment was based on false premises and the anachronistic standards of classic and romantic verse. One anachronism, however, may have heped: the asperities of some of the modern poets we admire. And indeed, we must always keep in mind that part of our strong attraction toward the seventeenth century may be a matter of elective affinities of a wide-spread and subtle kind.

With Fiske it becomes clear that, consciously or unconsciously, he sacrificed most of the adornment and sensuous attraction so generally characteristic of poetry, baroque or otherwise, in the service of another poetic principle that is more specifically baroque. He was interested not in the beautiful word or phrase or line, but in the formal composition of the whole and in the means for attaining a perfect interweaving of the parts into an intricate and integral unity. For this he developed a principle of composition about which the poetics of that time and since remain silent.

Of this principle of composition I can speak briefly since I shall go on to a practical demonstration that will perhaps serve better to clarify the whole matter. Fiske began with an anagram on the name of the person to be memorialized. In the pansophic world view, with its doctrine of signatures, such an outward sign pointed to an inner essence. The right anagram was, "cabalistically," a revelation of the inner nature of the name and its bearer and thus could properly be used as the theme of a poem. And with this came Fiske's creative next step that set him apart from the usual anagrammatist. He took the anagram as basic thematic material, paired or contrasted, and developed his poem contrapuntally around it. He thus composed his poems fugally, more in the musical than in the poetic tradition of the time. Here again it is significant for the change in taste of our times that nowadays many people like the old polyphonic music, whereas a half century or so ago few people beyond the musically trained could overcome their harmonic-melodic bias.

Perhaps Fiske's purest example of thematic interplay and mutation is his elegy on John Cotton, whom he anagrammatized as "O, Honie knott." This is, for the purpose, a really felicitous anagram, bringing out as it does the two salient features of this great spiritual leader: his personal charm and his subtle intelligence. Once the artistic principle is understood, it is a true joy to follow these motifs of the honey and the knot through the poem in all their intricate interweaving and variation and development. To be sure, the poem, with all the asperities of its period and technique, will never be popular, its virtuosities and subtleties will not readily be appreciated to the full, especially not if a rhetorical rather than a musical approach is taken to it. Nevertheless, one passage especially has been variously reprinted during the past decades, for in it Fiske offers an illuminating epigram on baroque aesthetics:

> The knot sometimes seems a deformity.
> It's a mistake, though such be light set by.
> The knot it is the joint, the strength of parts,
> The body's beauty. . . .

Only rarely is it possible to quote from such a poem, with its single, integral, continuous composition; and any attempt to find isolated "fine lines" would simply be an indication that one misunderstood its artistic nature.

Another poem, however, is eminently quotable, simply because it is only ten lines long, and at the same time a concentrated exemplar of the power and glory that this polyphonic technique can attain. It is anonymous but almost certainly by John Fiske, unless we make the improbable assumption that in this time and place there was another poet of such concentrated mastery. It was sent to old Governor Thomas Dudley in 1645. The anagram derived from the name was "Ah! old, must dye." And indeed the theme, image, and figure of "Memento mori" hover over the whole poem:

> A death's head on your hand you need not wear,
> A dying head you on your shoulders bear.
> You need not one to mind you, you must die,
> You in your name may spell mortality.
> Young men may die, but old men these die must.
> T'will not be long before you turn to dust,
> Before you turn to dust! ah! must; old, die!
> What shall young do when old in dust do lie?
> When old in dust lie, what New England do?
> When old in dust do lie, it's best die too.

The poem begins with the simple statement that the old governor needs no reminder from a death's-head ring when his very name is that reminder. For the old man, as not for the young, death is a "must," and the thematic "must die" leads on remorselessly to the rhymes "dust," "lie." These then, combined with the thematic "old," toll five times through the poem to its end, waiting after the second stroke for the four theme words, "ah! must; old, die!" to be intoned like the closing strokes of the death knell, and then vibrating through to the end. With the five and the four strokes of expiring time, the three aspects of time are memorialized in the three last lines: the old pioneers have passed, the young look forward to an uncertain future, the bleak present has no prospect but the dust of death. The five, the four, the three are reduced to two, to one, to a final sigh. It is one of the most carefully wrought poems of the period, deeply satisfying aesthetically, if one can transcend personal or temporal biases. Only repeated readings will do it full justice; a second reading will convey at least some intimations of its impressive poetic mastery:

> Thomas Dudley
> ah! old, must dye
> A death's head on your hand you need not wear,
> A dying head you on your shoulders bear.
> You need not one to mind you, you must die,
> You in your name may spell mortality.
> Young men may die, but old men these die must.
> T'will not be long before you turn to dust,
> Before you turn to dust! ah! must; old, die!
> What shall young do when old in dust do lie?
> When old in dust lie, what New England do?
> When old in dust do lie, it's best die too.

Our third representative poet, Edward Taylor, also had the vision of a poetic work of stature, perspective, and complex articulation, not in the form of an inspired epic (his epic attempt was hardly inspired), not in the form of a majestic fugue, but in the form of a lyric cycle, "God's Determinations," plumbing the mysteries of God's wondrous ways toward man.

Taylor was some thirty-five years younger than Fiske, forty-five than Johnson. He belongs to a new era, and his poems clearly show it. The poems are late baroque in their somewhat looser integration, in that the separate poems of the cycle can exist independently, and that even brief passages from these poems can effectively be quoted. And yet, there was the will to a higher integration, and even a certain power in achieving it in the somewhat less closely knit form of the poetic cycle. What we should pause to consider is that such a will and such an achievement were not at all usual in the period. Naturally, Donne, Herbert, and others had preceded Taylor in the writing of lyric religious cycles. Nevertheless, his was something different, in tone, modulation, transition, and variation. Just how different perhaps still remains to be analysed. Certainly, if there is to be a just interpretation and formal analysis of the work, its characteristics as a lyric cycle will have to be a central consideration.

This, however, would be a task in itself and not a matter for a few observations near the end of a lecture. In most other respects the poetry of Edward Taylor has been so fully and ably considered and it has become so well known that there is hardly any need for me to examine it except for the aspects in which it is representative of the American Baroque.

Among the early poems the elegy on John Allen contains some intimations of the future poet in its use of an odd, complex, though consistent set of images and its bizarre yet strangely appropriate choice of word and phrase. In his handling of language Taylor is one of the most original and creative of American poets, even though his all-too-great daring sometimes did lead to failure. Still more important is his ability to infuse abstract concepts, even theological dogmas, with the pulsating breath of life. In contrast to the few great poets who share this talent with him (Lucretius, Schiller, Shelley among them) Taylor does not generally provide a poetic incarnation on the same exalted level that the ideas occupy. His means for achieving this materialization is his rich store of images drawn from every phase of daily and Sunday life; he rather prefers than scorns to use the most homely or plebian image to embody the most exalted idea, and he will even use an occasional vulgarism if it suits his purpose.

Taylor employs his treasure of images in a typically late baroque manner: lavishly but purposefully and consequentially, in an ordered, well-disposed intricacy. His senses were extraordinarily acute, and his verse is replete with images of touch, smell, and taste, as well as of sight and hearing. He was apparently of a very passionate and sensuous nature, but, as with the older mystics, this was dominated by his intense religious yearning and sublimated to symbolic expression in the service of God. This is in contrast to Steere whose sensibilities were equally acute but who was convinced that God intended them to be realized, with moderation, in an earthly manner.

With Taylor, as with the other colonial poets of quality and substance, we need to exercise some caution as we try to assign to them their proper place in American literature. Though the general prejudices against the baroque are fast disappearing, the specific prejudices against American Baroque remain strong, partly because so much of the bad and so little of the good had been so long and so widely known. Once the effects of one hundred and fifty years of negative conditioning have worn off, once a better understanding of Taylor broadens into a better understanding of his contemporaries, these prejudices also will gradually abate.

The danger is, of course, that if we understand Taylor wrongly or inadequately, such misunderstanding could be transferred to the others. One danger lies in thinking of Taylor as a belated concettist. Concettism is a feature of late Renaissance Mannerism. Though the baroque took it over, it transformed it and subordinated it to its larger purposes. To see only the superficial ornamental features of the conceit and fail to see its function and integration in the whole, will mean missing the point and confusing the issue. Taylor's first editor truly saw the point of the poet's functional and integrated use of imagery, as we can infer from at least one statement (18): "By thus developing one single figure in a poem, Taylor avoids a fault to which almost all sacred poets are commonly prone, that is, of strewing metaphors throughout their verses with prodigal abandon." And Norman S. Grabo in his judicious study speaks even more tellingly to the point: "His strange ability to remind readers of others—from Clement of Alexandria to Walt Whitman—frees Taylor from the narrow designation 'metaphysical' and associates him with major writers in the entire stream of Christian, English, and American literature."

Under such good auspices the danger of misunderstanding would seem to be small. With the development of a precise terminology and careful distinctions, with the removal of still extant prejudices andconfusions, the way would seem clear to a true estimate of the period as a whole. That this could progress further into an overestimate, would seem unlikely. John Fiske is too difficult in form, Edward Johnson and even Edward Taylor are too difficult in attitude to have a wide appeal in our day. The best they can hope for is some measure of esteem for their poetic achievement, some recognition of their originality and creativity. It is to be remembered, of course, that originality is not always accompanied by quality. Independence only rarely leads to greatness, pioneer work only rarely is classic. This makes it all the more impressive that Taylor's first-hand imagery and personal diction were incorporated in several poems of true artistic quality, that Fiske's unprecedented venture into contrapuntal composition resulted in at least three poems of an austere aesthetic appeal even in our day (for those who understand them), and that Johnson's prophetic vision, epic power and expression rang out strongly in some of the noblest early passages on the founding of the American commonwealth.

My primary motive when I began work on *The First Century of New England Verse* was to conduct an experiment in literary history. I here had a probably unique opportunity of working in a time and region where only a fraction of the material had previously been known and evaluated, and of building up from these elemental beginnings and searchings through all the successive steps of grouping and organizing, of interpreting and evaluating, to the final synthesis revealing both an articulation and a course of development that could not have been predicted. I learned much about literary history in general, how it moves and goes through its gradual mutations. But I must confess, by way of conclusion, that my chief intellectual joy in this long labor was the by-product of a new acquaintance with a long row of writers, great and small, smooth and rough, conciliatory and cantankerous, original and imitative, and altogether human in their fallibility and aspiration. A literary scholar should at some time take a very close look at some limited period and region of literature; it will add much to his understanding of the few great men who came out of it.

Beyond all this, beyond the chief intellectual joy, there came to me a more precious human joy, that of the acquaintance, and friendship, with a remarkable group of young people, from all parts of the country and from abroad, who took me into their midst and allowed me to share with them the excitement of their new discoveries and new insights. They have been charitable in overlooking the lapses of a pioneer work and generous in acknowledging its contributions. What is more, they disregard the fact that I was no specialist, that

I had come over from another, neighboring field. They did so in the spirit of true liberalism that resists bureaucratic compartmentalization and maintains the ancient humanistic principle of free access to everything in life and art that arouses our sense of wonder and our urge to inquiry.

HAROLD JANTZ
THE JOHNS HOPKINS UNIVERSITY

NEW VOICES FROM

SEVENTEENTH-CENTURY AMERICA

It was in mid-October, a little over thirty years ago, that Harold Jantz's *The First Century of New England Verse* was published in the *Proceedings* of the American Antiquarian Society in Worcester, Massachusetts.

Oddly enough, this pioneering work went relatively unheralded until more than a decade after its first appearance, but in the late 1950s *The First Century* began to challenge students of early American literature, and by the time it was reprinted in 1962, it had achieved its deserved place on the working shelf of every scholar interested in the literature of early New England. In this volume we had for the first time a genuine base to work from in our effort to record all the titles of poems composed by Americans of the seventeenth century, to locate and identify the manuscript and various printed versions of these poems, and to begin the task of establishing authoritative texts.

Jantz himself provided the challenge. In his modest assessment of his own accomplishment, he wrote in the Introduction to *The First Century*:

> Anything like perfection is . . . a remote and unattainable
> ideal, and the best that can be hoped for is that finally enough

of the pertinent material has been gathered and arranged in such a way that the individual poems and poets can be seen in fairly correct perspective and that reasonably valid conclusions can be drawn (p. 6).

And he concluded:

From this point onward it is hoped that other students of the period will contribute corrections and supplementary material

After the holy Communion.

On Christmas day

Looke Sheapherds ! why ! where ?
see yee not yonder ! yonder ! There !
LORD ! what a glorious Light
streames through the aire !
Never was Sunne so bright
nor Morne so faire.
Methinkes it doth appeare
Like glory comeinge neare.

Listen Sheapherds, Listen round !
Harke ! heare yee not a sound ?
LORD what a heavenly noise
beats through the aire ?
Never was sweeter Voice,
nor Noate so cleare. !

Heavenly Musick ! Heavenly Musick !
Glorious Light ! Glorious Light !
Yet more fearfull, fearfull, fearfull, then the Night

Feare not Sheapherds, For behold !
Better Tydings ne're were told,
News wee bringe you this same tide
This blessed Morne
That to you, & all mankinde beside
a Saviour is Borne

Post to Bethlehem, post to Bethlehem, post about,
Post and finde the Infant out;
With these Signes you shall begin
In a Stable att an Inne,

in order to bring the work to a reasonably definitive state
(p. 6).

Though the "corrections and supplementary material" Jantz
invited in 1943 were not immediately forthcoming after *The
First Century* first saw print, they did finally begin to appear
—and then to increase in number to the extent, in fact, that
Professor Jantz is now preparing a new edition of *The First
Century* which will contain not the 1,000 titles by 175 known
poets and a few unknown ones that comprised the original
volume, but more than 2,200 titles by some 250 poets, known
and unknown.

That I have had some share in contributing certain of these
supplementary materials provides the focus for this paper.

To be sure, not all of the poets whose work will be recorded for the first time in the edition of *The First Century*
were adept at their craft. Benjamin Bartholomew, whose only
known poem may be found in the Harvard manuscript collection (MS. Am. 1302) under the title "A relation off the
wonderful Mercies off God Extended hereunto us yᵉ 19 off
October 1660 in the Ship Exchang being bound ffrom New-
england to Barbadoes," will be remembered not so much for
the quality of his verse as for his remarkable talent for reliving
the adventure he experienced when a fierce storm threatened
his ship, and relating that adventure dramatically. Successive
stages of action and emotion are recreated in the verse with
immediacy and suspense. After the storm has struck, the dis-
may with which the seamen see the shattered mainmast "beat
against the ship" and the desperation which causes the crew to
cast away "all that combered" are evoked vividly by Bartholomew:

> At foure a cloke winds dredffully did blow
> And as't grew night Sease higer still did growe
> [All] sailes butt mainsaille by us banded ware
> ffor dredfful wether we did greatly ffear

> Till at the last our rudor it did breake
> And in our quarter it did Make a leake
> Yett more and more the winds increased ware:
> We war almost at our wits end with feare
> And which much aded to our dolfull case
> then tenn foote watter in the hould there was
> Our Mison Mast we fain would have left stood
> butt seeing that it did more hurtt then good
> We did it cutt and cast into the sea:
> And what would we nott doe in misire.

Bartholomew was a staunch Puritan, as were the *Exchange's* seamen, and when it seemed inevitable that the ship was about to capsize and sink, some of the crew

> . . . went unto the master and did say
> All hopes of living longer's fleed away
> Theirfore whiles thatt we Live and whilst thatt we may
> Unto our God though Angery Lett us pray.

But the ship's master was a practical man as well as a god-fearing one:

> He then replied to pray I would aggree
> Yett for our Lives Lett all means used bee
> Therefore I think tis beast to hoyse fforeyarde
> Who knows butt God to us may have regard.

Prayer and practicality saved the day, for the *Exchange* rode out the storm and limped into port. Bartholomew concludes:

> O let this great deliverance we have passt:
> Reduce us from our sinns to god at last:
> Who our lives thretened yett did nott them end
> Iff this will not what will our lives amend [?]

Mrs. Mary English (née Hollingsworth) of Salem (1658–1694) wrote an ingenious acrostic memorializing her beloved husband Philip, and Mr. N. F. (so far known only by his initials) appended an acrostic in three four-line stanzas to his thirty-four quatrain "Elegy upon . . . Mr. John Huntting . . . April 12, 1689," preserved in a Brown University Library broadside. Sarah (Whipple) Goodhue composed one of the very few triolets surviving from this period in American literature to conclude her eleven-line poem recording the names and characters of her five children (1641–1681) born in Ipswich (*The Copy of a Valedictory* [Cambridge, Mass., 1681]). And Samuel Phillips of Andover wrote scurrilous verses on both Nicholas Noyes and George Curwen which are preserved in Evans #1924 and which moved the excitable Ichabod Wiswall, author of the longest poem of the period on the great comet of 1680, to respond in a twenty-six line query beginning, "Poor Man, what makes you look so sullen?"

Benanuel Bower of Scituate (ca. 1625–ca. 1695) joins the list of hitherto unrecorded writers of the century because of his thirty-six line verse epistle addressed to "Thomas Danforth, Maggistrate" and dated "From Cambridge Prison March 3, 1677." Danforth had been unremitting in his persecution of Quakers, and is reported by George Bishop in *New England Judged by the Spirit of the Lord* to have said to one Wenlock Christison, a Quaker,

> "Wenlock, I am a mortal man, and die I must, and that ere long, and I must appear at the tribunal-seat of Christ, and must give an account for my deeds in the body; and I believe it will be my greatest glory in that day, that I have given my vote for thee to be soundly whipped. . . ."

Earlier, a young Quaker woman, Deborah Wilson, walked through the town of Salem naked, "as a sign; which she having in part performed . . . was soon laid hands on, and brought before old Hathorne, who ordered her to appear at the next Court of Salem, at which your wicked rulers [Danforth and Daniel Goggin] sentenced her to twenty or thirty cruel stripes." Similarly treated was Miss Elizabeth Hooton, and when she was then "thrust into a noisome, stinking dungeon," Benanuel Bower, a "tender Friend," brought her "a little milk in this her great distress." Bower was then fined five pounds and imprisoned for "entertaining a stranger." For the ensuing fifteen years he and his wife were called to account almost annually and fined for some breach of church or public ordinance. When early in March 1677 he was again fined and imprisoned, he wrote to Danforth:

It is nigh hard this fifteene years since first
      our war begun
And yet the feild I have not lost nor thou the
      conquest wunn
Against thy power I have ingaged which of
      us twoo shall conquer
I am resolved if God assist to put it to
      the venter
Both my person and estate for truth Isle
      sacrafise
And all I have Ile leave at stake Ile venter
      winn or loose
He that from his cullors runs and leaves his
      captaine in the feild
By the law of armes he ought to dy and reason
      good should yeald
Unwise art thou against the streame to strive
For in thy enterprise thou art not like to thrive
Thy forces are to weake thou art not like to
      conquer
For with a power thou hast ingagd that will thy
      forces scatter
Of him thats wise thou counsell didst not take
Thy teachers like unto thyself Ime sorry for
      thy sake
Though of Christianity profession thou dost make

> And yet thy neighbor doest oppress only for
>   conscience sake
> Thou art as blind as Bonner was that burnt the
>   martyrs at the stake
> To the proud belongs the fall he surely shall
>   comm downe
> Out of his throne be brought he shall mans
>   pride must come to th ground
> Abomminable if be his deed soe in the end heas
>   like to speed
> Dread belongs to the evell Almighty God will
>   recompence[.]

Some 250 miles to the south, the Flushing, Long Island, Quaker leader John Bowne was having similar troubles with Peter Stuyvesant. Bowne, accused by Resolved Waldron, Sheriff of Flushing, of holding Quaker meetings at his farm, was brought before Stuyvesant for trial, was convicted, and fined 150 guilders and costs. When Bowne refused to accept his guilt, or the sentence, and further refused to remove his hat in deference to Stuyvesant's authority, this intransigence brought the inevitable result: banishment from the colony. Heartsick at having to leave his wife, his children, and his home, Bowne entered in his *Journal* a list of passages to read in the Bible as a comfort in time of distress, and concluded with a notably non-Quaker poetic lament:

> All though oure marterd bodyes
> In Earth heare silant lyes
> Oure righteous soules for ever liues—
> Our bloode still vengeance Cryes.
>   [*Journal*, MS. N.Y.H.S., Fol. 18^r]

When the Bowne case was brought before the Amsterdam Chamber, these practical burghers wrote Stuyvesant as follows:

Your last letter informed us that you had banished from the province and sent hither by ship a certain Quaker, John Bowne by name. Although we heartily desire that these other sectarians remained away from there [New Amsterdam], yet as they do not, we doubt very much whether we can proceed against them rigorously without diminishing the population and stopping immigration which must be favored at so tender a stage of the country's existence. You may therefore shut your eyes, at least not force people's consciences, but allow everyone to have his own belief, as long as he behaves quietly and legally, gives no offense to his neighbors and does not oppose the government. As the government of this city [Amsterdam] has always practiced this maxim of moderation and consequently has often had a considerable influx of people, we do not doubt that your Province too would be benefitted by it (H. H. Kessler and Eugene Rachlis, *Peter Stuyvesant and His New York* [New York: Random House, 1959], p. 196).

These manuscripts, and a good number more like them, are important not only because they add to our knowledge of seventeenth-century New England verse as we strive to make our census of these materials ever more complete, but also because they dramatize and illuminate specific historical events or points of view. In reference to these manuscripts, however, I have used the term *verse,* for it is clear that, with only an occasional exception, these additions to the census must be regarded principally as of historical rather than as of aesthetic value.

Such is *not* the case with the manuscript I want now to discuss, for I am convinced that this document, newly uncovered and described here for the first time, adds a dimension of genuine importance to the field.

Now among the holdings of the Rare Books Collection of The Pennsylvania State University Library is the 150-page autograph manuscript

GOSPELMANNA/ or / convenient Food for / them of riper age, who by reason / of vse have their senses exercised to /

discerne both good & evill. / Provided to Feed, nourish, &
strengthen/the Elder Lambs of Christ, and usefull/for such
as desire to be confirmed in / the Faith of christ's true Religion,
and / to be made fitt and worthy Receivers of / the most holy
sacrament of christ's / Bodie and BLOOD. / By David Dunster,
Prebendary / of Limricke, and sometime student / of Harvard
Colledge in New England / Anno 1683

A second title page, which follows page 32 in the ms., reads:

Eucharisticall / Exercises w[th] / MEDITATIONS, PRAYRS /
and / Severall other pious Devotions / upon diverse Duties, &
gestures / Before, At, & After the Blessed / communion / . . .
/ By David Dunster M.A. and / sometime Member of Harvarde / Colledge in New England. / . . . / Written by the
Author in / the Yeare. / 1683

Written in red and and black ink on small octavo gatherings,
each leaf measuring 3½″ x 6″ and crown watermarked, the
manuscript is bound in contemporary sombre morocco, gilt,
and unusually tightly sewn. It is organized into three sections
—of 34, 72, and 37 pages each (with seven blanks, some used
to enter unrelated genealogical data for the years 1684–1704).

The first thirty-two pages of the manuscript contain the
long "Gospelmanna," a dialogue between "Catecumen" and
"Catechist" in which "by way of Question and Answer is
laid downe the whole Doctrine of the Sacrament." In form,
style, and theme this dialogue is like many another preserved
in manuscript and in print from the seventeenth century. The
"Catecumen" begins:

S[r] When in my serious meditations I call to minde the pro-
found Mystery of the most holy Sacrament, and the necessity
that lyes upon mee to be made a Pertaker therof, together with
my owne Ignorance, & vnpreparednesse: I judge it needfull to
be better instructed before I adventure to goe to the Holy
Table, And in order thervnto, doe earnestly crave some of your
ghostly councell, & ministeriall advice.

The "Catechist" responds:

> That you shall freely have, and accordinge to ye measure of grace bestowed vpon mee, I shall informe you in each thinge you desire to be resolved in: wherfore you may proceed to make your demands.

Then, in familiar order, the Catecumen inquires about each of the duties and steps in preparation for partaking of communion, about the symbolic meaning of the various aspects of the ritual, and about the precise meanings of terms such as *original sin*, *grace*, and *conversion*. The Catechist responds to each query, sometimes with satisfying brevity but more often at length and in detail.

As an example of this familiar form, I suspect this dialogue ranks a cut or two above the ordinary, but it is by no means outstanding. And were this dialogue the only, or even the principal, matter of this manuscript, we should record it as being merely of passing interest. It is the remainder of the manuscript, with the title "Eucharisticall Exercises . . . Meditations, Prayrs," and particularly that part containing "Hymnes, Psalmes, & Anthemnes, &c.," that is of principal interest to us as students of early American poetry. Here are some sixty pages of verse, all on religious subjects and ranging in quality from clumsy to excellent, and in a variety of forms, from the simple quatrain in iambic or trochaic foot, in varying tetrameter and trimeter lines, to an elaborate four-part acrostic and a free "metaphrase" of the *Song of Songs*.

The first pages of poetry contain inauspicious verses.

All Glory Be to God on High

> All GLORY be to God on High,
> And PEACE on earth likewise;
> Good will to vs eternallie
> By CHRIST our Sacrifice.

Then to the Blessed Trinitie
   All praise & glory bee
Both now, henceforth, for evermore
   Amen, Amen say wee.

The songe of the Blessed Virgin

My Soule doth Magnifie the LORD
   My Spirit doth doe the same,
And all the powers that are in mee
   Ioy in my SAVIOURS Name.

.   .   .   .   .

To Him, therfore, and to his sonne
   with the blest Spir't of grace
Be glory, honour, power, ascribed
   by each succeeding race.

The quality improves as we come to Dunster's first "acrostick," on the phrase "None but Christe":

ACCROSTICKS
NONE BUT CHRISTE

Not Gold, nor Silver, Pearles, nor worldly pelfe
O Jesu Saviour! But thine owne deare selfe,
Not Life, or length of dayes, doe I desire;
Eternall Christ thou'rt that which I require.
But thee, but thee, sweet Jesu! none but thee
Unties the knott of my soules miserie
To the I come y^n none can me annoy
Convinc'd in thee is my ete[r]nal joy
How good in bless'd estate with thee to be
Receive me y^n, for I'le have none but the[e]
Iesus how sweet thou dost with glories shine
Satiate this soul y^t dost for Jesus pine
Thrice bless'd they whose thou art & whose are thine.

And by the time we read Dunster's first poem on the Nativity,
we are aware that this man is not just another writer of verse;
here is an original and imaginative poet.

On christmas day

Looke Sheapherds! Why? Where?
See yee not yonder! yonder! There!
LORD! what a glorious Light
streames through the aire!
Never was Sunne so bright
nor Morne so faire.
Methinkes it doth appeare
Like glory comeinge neare.

Listen Sheapherds, Listen round!
Harke! heare yee not a sound?
LORD what a heavenly noise
beats through the aire!
Never was sweeter Voice,
nor Noate so cleare!
Heavenly Musick! Heavenly Musick!
Glorious Light! Glorious Light!
Yet more fearfull, fearfull, fearfull, then the Night.

Feare not, Sheapherds; For behold!
Better Tydings, ne're were told,
News wee bringe you this same tide
This blessed MORNE
That to you, & all mankinde beside
a Saviour is Borne.

Post to Bethlehem, post to Bethlehem, post about,
Post and finde the Infant out;
With these Signes, you shall begin,
In a Stable att an Inne,

You shall finde his Mother Maide
poorly Friended
And the BABE in a manger laid
worse attended.

When you finde Him loudly Crie
Glory be to GOD on high.
Glory be to GOD above
Peace on Earth; & to Men, Love.

Death, and Hell, are now beguiled
GOD, and Men, are reconciled.
Hallelujah! Hallelujah!
Hallelujah! Hallelujah!

The author of this manuscript was David Dunster, born 16 May 1645, the eldest of five children, two of whom died in infancy. David's father was Henry Dunster, second president of Harvard College, whose term of office came to an unhappy end in October 1654, after fourteen years at his post, as the result of a controversy in which Dunster refused to relax his opposition to infant baptism. Dunster, indeed, was found guilty of "disturbance of the ordinances of Christ uppon the Lord's daye" for having preached publicly against infant baptism, and was later fined for not permitting his own children to be baptized.

Perhaps because Henry fell from Harvard's grace when his oldest son was still very young, it is probable that David acquired his education privately, rather than at Harvard as he here twice claims on the two title pages of *Gospelmanna*. In 1662, three years after Henry's death, Elizabeth Dunster, his widow and David's mother, wrote that she had disbursed £100 for David's education over a three-year period, much more than a full term at Harvard would have cost, and she refers specifically to David's "excellent and costly" training.

Obviously, private tutoring is suggested, particularly because David Dunster's name is nowhere to be found in the generally complete records of Harvard's entrants and graduates. The author of *Gospelmanna*, therefore, seems to have prevaricated on his title page. And I must add: not for the last time.

In 1662, at age seventeen, David's career—at whatever stage it had reached at that time—was climactically interrupted. He was found guilty in General Court of fornication and bastardy, having impregnated a neighbor's servant girl, Jane Bowen. Young Dunster was sentenced "to pay a fine of £20 to the use of the County, or to be whipt, and also to give £50 bond with sufficient securities for defraying the charges" (for court costs, for the lying-in expenses, and for care of the infant). This public disgrace, almost certainly exacerbated in a community that well recalled his father's stern stand on infant baptism, occasioned his mother's decision to pack the lad off to England with £50 in his pocket to begin a new life. Jane Bowen was sentenced to be "severely whipt. 20 stripes," and to be imprisoned at hard labor until otherwise provided for or claimed. The infant was taken from her and delivered into the keeping of the Dunster family.

The ensuing fourteen years in David Dunster's life remain, after some months of record-seeking and probing, somewhat of a biographical blank which I hope to fill by further research. But in 1676, David, now 31, was installed as Prebendary of Kilpeacon in the Chapter of St. Mary's Cathedral, Limerick. In this post he remained two years, but in 1678 he was discharged as "incapable of serving and absent beyond the Kingdom." It is possible that the phrase "beyond the Kingdom" meant that Dunster had returned to New England, but at the time of his death eighteen years later, in 1695/96, he was almost certainly in England. Furthermore, he was not Prebendary of Limerick in 1683, any more than he was a "sometime member of Harvarde Colledge in New England," and no institution empowered to grant an M.A. recorded having con-

ferred this degree upon Dunster. Thus, the three credentials
the author of *Gospelmanna* claims upon his two title pages
are, to say it in the most generous way, certainly less than
the truth.

Add this further bit of confusion: in 1696, Rowland Cotton,
having just graduated from Harvard, visited England and,
according to David's sister, wrote a letter received by the
Dunsters on 3 July informing "her of the death of her brother
Doctor David Dunston [sic]."

It would appear, at this point, that Thomas Morton was
not the only seventeenth-century American miscreant, though
of course records may yet come to light to resolve some of the
numerous discrepancies and contradictions so far apparent in
this incomplete record of the life of David Dunster. There can
be little question, on the other hand, that this manuscript is of
key importance in the canon of early American poetry.

Of the approximately 250 poets we can identify in this era,
roughly half of that number are represented by a single extant
work, in some cases merely a stray couplet or quatrain that
has survived. A Urian Oakes in this company is verily *rara
avis*. Of the remaining hundred, we can count barely a score
for whom we have substantial amounts of their poetry available
to us: Taylor, Bradstreet, Wigglesworth, Sewall, Saffin, Steere,
and Cotton Mather, for example. If for no other reason, then,
than the sheer amount of his work preserved in this manuscript, David Dunster takes his place as an important figure
in this company.

But Dunster is more than that. His poems in celebration of
the Nativity are the earliest we have record of in American
literature, in their composition antedating by some years
Richard Steere's "Upon the Cælestial Embassy Perform'd by
Angels." His long poem on Saint Stephen's Martyrdom is the
only one on that subject extant from the era, and its triplet
form, two heroic couplets followed by an alexandrine, is
unique, I think, in early American verse. Dunster experi-

mented with varied verse forms, occasionally employing several different line lengths and stress patterns even within a single stanza. His poem "Cease Rachell, cease to weep" begins:

> Cease Rachell, cease to weep, but rather Sing
> Thy children dy'd true subjects of theire King
> And Martyrs too, a far more blessed thing.
> And are
> Instated there
> In Glory vast and great
> Wher neither Herod, Time, nor cruell Fate
> Theire Souls can kill, themselves exasperate
> But they shall be
> From all mischevious cancred malice free
> To all Eternitie.
>
> Where such grand massacrees there shall be none
> Nor shall grim face of Murderers be known
> Or heard shall ther be either sigh or groane
> of wand
> Sad parents and
> of dying Infants skreeks
> No poniard, speare, nor sword, or wound y^t reaks
> With the warme blood which from sad gashes leeks
> And makes the ground
> T' appeare like a red sea about it round
> Shall evermore be found.

But it is in Dunster's metaphrase of the *Song of Songs* that we have his best poetry. Imaginative, well-conceived, well-executed, the individual poems which as a group constitute Dunster's most sustained poetic effort may be quite legitimately compared to Edward Taylor's series of meditations on the same text.

In certain respects, Dunster's poetics differ from Taylor's. Throughout the *Preparatory Meditations* Taylor uses the

pentameter line and organizes his poems into six-line stanzas.
Dunster experiments with trimeter, tetrameter, pentameter,
and occasional hexameter lines, and he regularly varies the
number of lines in stanzas. Dunster is less allusive than Taylor, nowhere using the "catalogue" technique Taylor favors
in such Meditations as 2.56, with its list of mechanical and
architectural wonders, or 2.67[B] with its rehearsal of physical illnesses traceable to original sin. Taylor frequently moves
outside the mainstream of the language, with such coinages
or dialectical words as *bedotcht*, *brudled*, *glout*, *snick-snarls*,
and *an hurden haump*, making readers grateful to Donald
Stanford's extensive glossary in the Yale *Taylor*. Only occasionally does Dunster startle his reader with word choice—
skreek, *swathband*, and *ubiquitic* the only examples I could
cull from 60 pages of poetry.

In many more ways, the two poets are alike. Because, however, many of us are knowledgeable about early American
poetry in general and certainly familiar with Taylor's *Meditations* in particular, I propose not to detail these similarities.
Instead, let me allow Dunster to speak for himself.

Here are two of his best occasional poems, "On Advent"
and "For Christmas Day," and four individual poems from
the metaphrase of *Canticles*.

On Advent

Lord Jesu come away,
Why dost thou so long stay?
  Thy Road is ready, & Thy Paths straight
  With Longing expectation waite
The Consecration of thy beauteous Feet.
  Ride on Triumphantly, behold wee Lay
  Our Lusts & proud wills in thy way.
Hosannah! Welcome to our hearts. Lord, here
  Thus hast a Temple too, and full as deare
As that of Zion; & as full of Sinne;

For nought but Theivees, & Robbers dwell therin:
The world, Sinne, Satan, Flesh, all they
   And many more, steall what wee have away.
Enter, & chase them forth; and cleanse the Floor;
Scourge, crucifie them, that never they may more
     Prophaine that mansion place,
  Which with thy holy Spirit thou dost grace.
   And then if our stiff tongues shall be
  Mute in the praises of thy Deity,
  The Stones out of the Temple wall
    Shall cry aloud, shall sing, & call
Hosanna! & thy glorious footsteps greet.
  The gentle neighborhood of grove & spring,
  Of streets, & lanes, shall burst forth ecchoing
Hosanna to King Davids sonne, & the highest
  Palme, shall be stript to strew thy way
Yea, all with one consent shall shout and say
BLEST be HEE that in Gods name, today
    to us doth come
  Hosanna! in the highest.

For christmas day

Wonders of wonders, Mysterie of Mysteries!
    That the selfe same should bee
A Lamb, a Shepherd, and a Lion, too!
    Yet such an one as HEE
    Whome first the Shepherds knew,
    When they themselves became
    SHEEP to the Shepherd-Lamb.
Shepherd of Men, and Angels, Lamb of God;
Lion of Judah; by these titles keep
The Wolfe from both thy Lambs & sheep
    Bringe all the world into thy fold;
    Let Jewes & Gentiles thither come

In numbers great that can't be told,
And call thy wandring pet-Lambs home,
Glory be to God on high,
All glories to th' glorious Deity
To Father, Sonne, and Holy Spirit
To the Triune that doth inherit
The dreadfull Throne, be Honour, praise,
Dominion, Glory, now, henceforth, & alwaise.

Christ

Am I so sweet, so Dear (my choisest Love)
Dost Thou my Person, excellent approove?
Nothing is lost: For Thou art unto Mee
Like Bunch of Camphire in faire Engedi.
More Faire, more Faire, (My Love) behold more Faire!
Thy sparkling Eyes, like harmlesse Doves eyes are;
Behold Thou'rt Faire (My Love) I have not seen
Any so Pleasant. Lo! our Bed is green.
Th' Beames of Our House, are all of Cedar sweet
And its faire Rafters made of Fir compleat.
I am the Blushing Rose of Sharon's Feild
I am the Lilly flower, which valleys yeild,
As amongst Thornes the Lily-sweet doth grow
So is my love amongst the Daughters too.

Christ his Invitation

Arise, Arise, my Fairest Love
Come, come, away
T'is I that call, Tis I my Deare
that calls I say
Now, now's the time of our delight.
For Lo! the Winter passed is
Th' raine's overgonn

The Flowers appear upon the Earth,
    Bird-singings come
Each pleasant thinge doth us invite.
The Turtledove with her sweet voice
    is heard and seen,
The Fig-tree causeth forth to Springe
    Her Fruit so green.
O let mee see that Face of Thine.

    The vines also with tender grapes
        Smell sweet I say.
    Arise, Arise, my Fairest One,
        Come, come, away.
Thou art the choisest Heart of mine.

My Dove in the Rocky clefts, close stairs
    O let Mee heare
Thy Voice; and see Thy Face, for They
    are Sweet, and Faire.
Then which nothing more Pleasant, cleare.
    Take us the Foxes take for us
        the Foxes all
    That spoile the vines, because our Vines
        are yet but small,
And they doe tender-grapes but beare.

Church

Whilest that the King in his bright Majestie
With Mee at's Table sate, immediately
I caus'd my spicknard (which was redolent)
For to breath forth its Aromatick scent;
Like to a pack of Precious Myrrhe, so is
My welbelov'd to mee. Those cheeks of his

Through all the Night betwixt my breasts shall lye
For sweet's himselfe, & Dears his Company.

Church Glorieth in Christ

Who's This that from
   the desert wildernesse doth come
      (like Smoakie Pillars Bright
Perfum'd with Myrrh,
   and each rich fragrant dust) to Her?
      Whist! Tis my Souls delight.
See where Hee lies, The Bed Hee rests upon
Is the royall Pallat of King Solomon

His Guards doe stand
   (Threscore most valiant in the Band)
      About him for to keep
His Life from harme;
   The Choise & best of Israels arme
      Attend my Love asleep.
They all hold Swordes, & are expert in warr
Each man prepar'd; Because of Nights darke fear.

King Solomon
   of th' fragrant wood of Lebanon
      For his owne selfe hath made
A chariot
   so rich, it ne're can be forgot
      for Studds it Silver had,
The Bottom pav'd with Plates of massie Gold,
And glorious Topp, did Tyrian Purple hold.

The Center Love,
   Zions Faire Virgins hearts to move.
      Behold! Him therin ride

Triumphantly.
  O Daughters of our Neat Citie
  Come forth; behold beside

This Glorious King, in his Imperiall state,
Crown'd with the Crown, w^{ech} his one Mother sate
Upon his Head, In that same Day that Hee
With Joy, & Gladnesse, was betroath'd to Mee.

One comes away from a reading of Dunster's manuscript with several clear impressions. Unquestionably here is a young poet striving to learn his craft. There are clumsinesses, to be sure, and commonplaces. Tag rimes appear too frequently, and too frequently Dunster leaves us with the uneasy feeling that he has spent too much time counting syllables. Meter stumbles, despite this counting, and the pat phrase disappoints where careful diction is demanded. These faults recognized and admitted, there rings through the best of Dunster's work the clear sound of a true poetic voice. I hope it is not only my enthusiasm, born at least in part out of my delight in discovery and still fresh after many months of working on this manuscript, that encourages me to name David Dunster not only as a new voice from seventeenth-century New England but also as a poet to rank well up the scale in the canon of early American literature.

HARRISON T. MESEROLE
THE PENNSYLVANIA STATE UNIVERSITY

THE STRUCTURE OF

ANNE BRADSTREET'S *TENTH MUSE*

The rehabilitation of Anne Bradstreet's reputation as a poet of importance, begun some four decades ago by Conrad Aiken's inclusion of a handful of her poems in his *American Poetry, 1671–1928,* has in our time become an accomplished fact. After a number of excellent essays in interpretation and two book-length studies,[1] she now stands firmly established as one of two major American Puritan poets, and if her gifts are on the whole not as rich as Edward Taylor's, her careful workmanship and her comparative freedom from rigid Puritan doctrines enable her, on occasion, to snatch a grace beyond the reach of his rougher and more theologically oriented art. Outside the realm of criticism, John Berryman's *Homage to Mistress Bradstreet* has done much to stimulate a rereading of her verse among those who should have re-read it long ago. Predictions always involve an element of chance, of course, but it seems unlikely that any serious student of American literature will in the future withhold from her, as nineteenth-century critics too often did, the "thyme or parsley wreath" she requested in her "Prologue" as a token of her genuine poetic achievement.

All this has been achieved perhaps the only way it could

have been, by ignoring more than one half of her total output and, in particular, by viewing the 1650 *Tenth Muse* almost exclusively as an historical edition; only "The Prologue" has consistently been accorded the respect of being reprinted in American Literature anthologies. Occasionally, some brave soul includes the elegy on Queen Elizabeth or twenty or so lines from "Spring" of "The Quaternions." For the rest, editors of anthologies and critics agree in centering on a group of a dozen or, at most, fifteen personal and religious poems not published until the posthumous 1678 edition prepared by John Rogers, the poet's nephew-in-law. Samuel Eliot Morison seems to speak for all when he writes: " 'The Tenth Muse' is not attractive. No one of its long poems, The Four Elements, The Four Humours of Man, The Four Ages of Man, The Four Seasons, The Four Monarchies, and A Dialogue between Old New England [sic] and New, would be read by anyone save a literary historian." [2]

The purpose of the present paper is not to disagree with Morison's evaluation of the poems in the earliest version of Anne Bradstreet's book, but rather to provide a corollary statement: *The Tenth Muse* is far more impressive, finally, when it is considered as a unit than when we isolate individual poems for analysis. In the case of "The Quaternions," indeed, it is certain that the poems were intended to be read together, and only when they are can we fully understand and appreciate their author's achievement. And we can, I think, go further, taking John Woodbridge's advice (and hint?) in his "Epistle to the Reader" of the 1630 edition. "I found," Woodridge says there, "that divers had gotten some of the scattered papers, affected them wel, [and] were likely to have sent forth broken peices [sic] to the Authors prejudice, which I thought to prevent, as well as to pleasure those that earnestly desired the view of the whole." [3] In this "view of the whole," Anne Bradstreet's poems, whatever the mediocrity of their rhymes and couplets in isolation, turn out to be closely inter-

connected thematically and, at times, imagistically as well.
The interrelationships established among apparently unrelated
pieces provide *The Tenth Muse* with a complexity which
has previously gone undiscerned and which makes the book
more valuable, both as literary history and as poetry, than
generations of critics seem to have suspected.

The best way to approach the thematic structure of *The
Tenth Muse* is indirectly, by listening to the voices which
Bradstreet employs in the three different sections of the work.
The initial three poems—"To Her Most Honoured Father,"
"The Prologue," and "The Quaternions" (this last comprised
of four separate poems)—constitute the first division. In
these the poet deprecates her wits and verse, and she readily
grants the superiority of the male in nearly all arenas of life.
The second division, consisting of "The Four Monarchies"
and "A Dialogue Between Old and New England," features an
ironic voice which is also characteristically Puritan—sometimes stridently so, as on her declamations against the Pope
and the Roman Catholic Church. The content of these two
poems is largely political, either implicitly or explicitly. In
addition, "The Four Monarchies" functions to balance the
easy surrender to masculine virtues in the first section, for
insofar as it is mostly an extended criticism of kings and political institutions men have invented, it suggests a questioning
of the political acumen and simple human wisdom of a succession of male potentates.[4] Finally, as a third division, there
is a small group of elegies and epitaphs in several of which the
author speaks with distinctly unpuritan tones, asserting that
man's accomplishments may win him fame and a form of
immortality.[5] But, as if uneasy with this concept, particularly
as a final statement for her book, she balances her heterodox
poems in praise of fame against two orthodox ones, "Davids
Lament for Saul and Jonathan" and "The Vanity of All
Worldly Creatures," and so concludes her *Tenth Muse*.

I

The dedicatory poem to Anne Bradstreet's father, Thomas Dudley, which begins *The Tenth Muse*, need not, strictly speaking, perform any function other than the one of paying a compliment to her parent. Yet, possibly because the daughter was inspired to try her own hand at verse-making by reading her father's now lost poem on the four parts of the world, it does much more than that. It introduces the subject matter of her "Quaternions" and states the theme that, in various ways, may well be considered the overriding theme of all her poetry, early and late: "How divers natures, make one unity" (p. 2).[6] Additionally, it marks the poet's first mention of du Bartas—Nathaniel Ward and an anonymous anagrammizer had linked her name with the French poet's earlier, in the testimonial verses—and thus looks forward, though distantly, to the elegy that comes near the end of the book. Most importantly, in "To Her Most Honoured Father," Mistress Bradstreet speaks in the voice which we hear throughout the first section of *The Tenth Muse*. She twice concedes the superiority of male poets, once to du Bartas—"I honour him, but dare not wear his wealth" (p. 2)—and once to her father:

I bring my four; and four, now meanly clad,
To do their homage unto yours most glad,
Who for their age, their worth, and quality,
Might seem of yours to claime precedency;
But by my humble hand thus rudely pen'd
They are your bounden handmaids to attend. (p. 1)

And, if that is not adequate for the male ego, she also discredits her own efforts, insisting that her "goods are true (though poor)" (p. 2). There is no biographical reason to doubt Bradstreet's sincerity or to question the genuineness of her humility, but a complete reading of *The Tenth Muse* reveals that there is more to the story.

Structurally, the next poem, "The Prologue," divides in
half at the end of the fourth stanza. The first four verses
abound in allusions to males—du Bartas appears again, in the
company of Demosthenes—and to masculine activities: war-
fare, the founding of commonwealths, public oratory, and
so on. In the second part of the poem, Bradstreet contrasts
these masculine endeavours with the small scope for action
customarily allotted to women in society—sewing and other
household chores—and attempts to establish woman's right to
be a poet. She argues from Greek myth that the writing of
poetry by women is appropriate because, after all, the Muses
are female. But again she gives in to the spectre of du Bartas
and his masculine counterparts. "Men can doe best, and
Women know it well" (p. 4), she says, and closes the poem
with an image of "glistering gold," metallurgical emblem of
the male and, incidentally, the perfect mineral. Only gold
contains all four elements in balance. Thus, unwittingly or
not, in the last line of "The Prologue," Bradstreet prepared
the way for the next poem, "The Foure Elements."

After a brief prologue of its own in which the chaotic consequences of an argument among the elements are depicted,
"The Foure Elements" begins with Fire as the first speaker.
Of the "Quaternions," this and the next poem, "Of the Foure
Humours in Mans Constitution," form a tight unit in their
essential circularity. As Fire commences hostilities, "Flegme,"
offspring of Water, ends them, and the circle which the contrast of speakers implies finds reinforcement in the imagery of
Phlegm's final speech:

> Unlesse we 'gree, all fals into confusion.
> Let Sanguine, Choler, with her hot hand hold,
> To take her moyst, my moistenesse wil be bold;
> My cold, cold Melanchollies hand shal clasp,
> Her dry, dry Cholers other hand shal grasp;
> Two hot, two moist, two cold, two dry here be,

A golden Ring, the Posey, *Unity:*
Nor jars, nor scoffs, let none hereafter see,
But all admire our perfect amity;
Nor be discern'd, here's water, earth, aire, fire,
But here's a compact body, whole, entire:
This loving counsel pleas'd them all so wel,
That Flegme was judg'd, for kindness to excel. (p. 40)

Both of these poems, "The Foure Elements" and "Of the Foure Humours," proceed by charge and counter-charge, as each speaker tries to prove her superiority to her sister and to refute her rival's interpretation of her character. They are thus tightly organized logically, and the logical structure even generates patterns of imagery which, if not highly original or metaphorically complex, nevertheless link each humor to its element and provide unity for the debate by filling the two poems with flaming figures, militaristic tropes, and other image clusters. The unity achieved by this method resembles, of course, the unity of baroque musical compositions and reminds us, perhaps more forcefully than her historical allusions do, of the century in which Anne Bradstreet was writing. Not only Edward Taylor but also his American predecessor created versions of colonial baroque.[7]

The remaining two poems of "The Quaternions," "The Four Ages of Man" and "The Four Seasons of the Yeare," are related in obvious ways to the first two, most importantly as parts of the quartet structure that the total work feaures. The second of the poems, "The Four Seasons," is also built around the image of a circle, as the first two Quaternions are, for "Winter" ends with an anticipation of spring as "In *Pisces* now the golden Sun doth shine,/And North-ward stil approaches to the Line" (p. 64). But "The Four Ages of Man" develops lineally around a metaphor possibly borrowed from Shakespeare, the comparison of the periods of man's life to acting on a stage, and it appears to draw most of its iconogra-

phy from emblem literature—Childhood enters bearing an
hour-glass, for instance—and, in the case of Old Age, from
Ecclesiastes. Neither in "The Four Ages of Man" nor in "The
Four Seasons" do we find the technique of argumentation, and
consequently the parts of the poem bear a less intricate formal
relationship to one another than was true of the first two
"Quaternions."

On the other hand, to the extent that the four seasons correspond to the four stages in man's career, the last two
"Quaternions" resonate upon one another and are emotionally
and metaphorically, rather than strictly logically, related.
Youth's "goodly cloathing" and "beauteous skin" (p. 46) finds
its counterpart in "Spring's Garments fine" (p. 57). The pastoral interlude in "Summer," where shepherds, "Carelesse of
worldly wealth" (p. 60), sit and pipe, stands in contrast to
Middle Age's complaints about the responsibilities of Manhood. The rich ripeness of "Autumne," as the year comes to
fruition, though superficially different from the sere and yellow leaf of Old Age, suggests the sentiment which the old
man who personifies Old Age expresses as he contemplates
death:

> It's not my valour, honour, nor my gold,
> My ruin'd house, now falling can uphold. . . .
> But what I have done wel, that is my prop;
> He that in youth is godly, wise, and sage,
> Provides a staffe for to support his age. (p. 53)

For both man and nature, autumn is a time of harvesting
the fruits that were sown in the spring of life. And as "Autumne" anticipates "Winter," which in turn closes with an
anticipation of the return of spring, so human life is contained
within the cycle of birth-death-rebirth. In this way, the
pastoral "Four Seasons" provides a restatement in naturalistic
terms of the faith in immortality which sustains Old Age as
he faces his own dissolution and death.

After Winter has had his say, the first portion of *The Tenth Muse* ends with a brief *apologia* which recalls the self-deprecating and submissive tone of "To Her Most Honoured Father" and the "Prologue":

> *My Subjects bare, my Brains are bad,*
> *Or better Lines you should have had;*
> *The first fell in so naturally,*
> *I could not tell how to passe't by:*
> *The last, though bad, I could not mend,*
> *Accept therefore of what is penn'd,*
> *And all the faults which you shall spy,*
> *Shall at your feet for pardon cry.* (p. 64)

Conspicuously absent from this apology, however, is any mention of innate feminine incapacity to write. Instead, the poet speaks with a critic's rather than a woman's voice. The appended *apologia* thus provides a bridge to the second section of *The Tenth Muse*, the portion in which Bradstreet, probably without full awareness of all her implications, tries a succession of male rulers—kings, emperors, and princes—at the tribunal of history and finds them all wanting.[8] Their failures loom even larger when measured against the glorious successes of Queen Elizabeth, but those are reserved for treatment in the third and final section.

II

Of all the verses in the first part of *The Tenth Muse*, none so clearly adumbrates the tone and content of the poems in the second grouping, "The Four Monarchies" and "A Dialogue Between Old and New England," as "Old Age." There is a distant foreshadowing of the criticism of monarchies in the pastoral interlude of "Summer," where, in keeping with pastoral conventions, Bradstreet holds up the simple life of shepherds as the envy of kings and notes that monarchs are always

"imbroyl'd in Wars" (p. 60), but only Old Age speaks with
the historical consciousness that informs "The Four Monarchies" and the "Dialogue." And his voice becomes distinctly
Puritan as he weaves the imagery and the sentiments of
Ecclesiastes into his final assessment of human strivings:

> From King to begger, all degress shal finde
> But vanity, vexation of the minde. (p. 55)

This biblical wisdom, in combination with the popular concept of the Wheel of Fortune and the advantages of a long
historical perspective, determines the ironic voice of the nar-
rator of "The Four Monarchies." In any overview of the rise
and fall of monarchs, nothing is so certain, from all three of
these points of view, as that

> . . . Kings stand,
> Now up, now down, as fortune turns her hand. . . . (p. 88)

This knowledge imparts a pervasive irony to the campaigns
and conquests of every ruler Mistress Bradstreet treats. Indeed, the greater the monarch, the greater the irony. From a
seventeenth-century perspective, the accomplishments of ancient kings seem far less significant than they did to the rulers
themselves. Thus, on page 120, in one of many similar au-
thorial intrusions, Bradstreet observes of Philip of Macedonia:
"(For as worlds Monarch, now we speak not on,/But as the
King of little *Macedon*)." But from an eternal perspective,
God's vantage point, even Alexander the Great's conquests are
trivial and without meaning, as the poet notes in lines that echo
both Ecclesiastes and Revelation:

> Thus Kings, and Kingdoms, have their times, and dates,
> Their standings, over-turnings, bounds, and facts;
> Now up, now down, now chief, and then brought under,
> The Heavens thus rule, to fill the earth with wonder.
> The *Assyrian* Monarchy long time did stand,

But yet the *Persian* got the upper hand;
The *Grecian*, them did utterly subdue,
And Millions were subjected unto few:
The *Grecian* longer than the *Persian* stood,
Then came the *Romane*, like a raging flood.
   .   .   .   .   .   .

The first a Lion, second was a Beare,
The third a Leopard, which four wings did rear;
The last more strong, and dreadful, than the rest,
Whose iron teeth devoured every beast.
   .   .   .   .   .   .

But yet this Lion, Bear, this Leopard, Ram,
All trembling stand, before that powerfull Lambe.
  (pp. 173–174)

These last lines suggest that Bradstreet viewed the four monarchies she chronicles in her poem as types of the power of Christ the King, who, as antitype, cancels out the significance of Assyrian, Persian, Greek, and Roman rulers by establishing an eternal kingdom of unlimited dominion. Even Death, the conqueror of conquerors, is subject to this last, greatest king. Meanwhile, the *vanitas vanitatum* theme applies, and Bradstreet's awareness of the wisdom of Koheleth determines nearly all of her judgments about kings and their kingdoms. There is, additionally, another source of pervasive irony in her treatment of kings and kingly ambitions. The last lines of "The Four Monarchies" as they appear in the 1650 edition report the decision of the Roman people "ne're to accept of King" (p. 179), which leaves us back where we began—not in an innocent Golden Age, perhaps, but at least in a country without kings. Thus all the efforts exerted by monarchs between Ninrod and Tarquinius Superbus to maintain supremacy over their subjects have produced nothing in the end, for the people insist upon their own sovereignty. Of course to view matters in this way requires us to overlook a great deal

of subsequent history, but the point is that, in the context of
Bradstreet's poem as she gives it to us in the 1650 *Tenth Muse*,
the lust for power of all earthly monarchs is contained within
both human and divine boundaries, circles beyond which no
king has power to go.

For the most part, Bradstreet seems content to exploit only
the irony inherent in the differences between a proximate,
immediate view of events and the long historical and Christian
vision, but there are notable exceptions. In "Alexander the
Great," for instance, the first part of "The Third Monarchy"
and the longest single poem in *The Tenth Muse*, she appears
to have sought a way to unify her disparate historical materials
—her chief sources were Plutarch, Curtius, and Seneca—and
to underscore the vanity of a hunger for power and empire in
the exploits of even the greatest of all conquerors of antiquity.
Accordingly, she structures her poem around the additional
irony of the conqueror who cannot conquer himself, a theme
succinctly expressed in one couplet:

> As *Alexander* in his greatnesse growes,
> So daily of his vertues doth he lose. (p. 136)

Bradstreet may have had in mind here the central Christian
question, propounded in Matt. 16:26, Mark 8:36, and Luke
9:25 (the last is the version quoted): "For what is a man ad-
vantaged, if he gain the whole world, and lose himself, or be
cast away?" Or she may have found the structural pattern of
material success counterpointed by spiritual and ethical decline
implicit in Plutarch. Whatever her sources, however, she made
good use of the dramatic irony suggested by the pattern.

The man who stands in contrast to Alexander and whose
career inverts the pattern of apparent rise-actual fall that con-
trols Bradstreet's presentation of the Greek conqueror is the
last monarch of Persia, Darius Codomanus. As she sketches his
story at the end of "The Second Monarchy," Bradstreet seems

to have been looking ahead to using Darius as a dramatic foil
to Alexander, for she explains:

That this *Darius* was last *Persian* King,
Whose warres and losses we may better tell;
In *Alexanders* reign who did him quell,
How from the top of worlds felicity;
He fell to depths of greatest misery,
Whose honours, treasures, pleasures, had short stay;
One deluge came, and swept them all away. . . . (p. 118)

Building upon this almost medieval concept of the Wheel
of Fortune and its revolutions, "Alexander the Great" goes on
to present Darius initially as a haughty and foolish ruler who
thinks to overawe the invading Greek legions by a display of
numerical superiority and wealth. An exchange of letters between him and Alexander as Alexander's armies overcome first
one and then another of his provinces indicates that loss of
property and empire has an ennobling effect upon Darius.
Finally, bereft of all treasures and betrayed by one of his own
men, Bessus, Darius becomes an object of the reader's (and,
one suspects, the poet's) sympathy. Wounded by Bessus and
left to die, Darius, sounding a good deal like Old Age in that
earlier poem, gives expression to the *vanitas vanitatum* theme
of "The Four Monarchies":

Of all good things (quoth he) once in my power,
I've nothing left, at this my dying houre. (p. 135)

Other monarchs—Porus, the Indian king, for example—also
serve as foils to Alexander insofar as they, too, are nobler in
defeat than he is in victory. In the same way, Alexander's chief
lieutenant, Parmenio, functions initially to indicate the difference between mere talent for conquest and true military
genius. When Darius first sues for peace and offers generous
concessions, Parmenio advises his commander that, were he

Alexander, he would accept the terms. Alexander's reply—
"And so, if I *Parmenio* were, would I" (p. 127)—simultaneously measures his greatness and his vaingloriousness. As success follows success, vainglory becomes his dominant character
trait, and he finally orders Parmenio slain, after first disposing
of Parmenio's son, Philotas:

> But how these Captaines should, or yet their Master,
> Look on Parmenio, after this disaster,
> They knew not; wherefore, best now to be done,
> Was to dispatch the Father, as the Son.
> This sound advice, at heart, pleas'd *Alexander,*
> Who was so much engag'd, to this Commander,
> As he would ne're confesse, nor could reward.
> .   .   .   .
> This is *Parmenio*, which so much had done,
> For *Philip* dead, and his surviving Son,
> Who from a petty King of *Macedon,*
> By him was set upon the *Persian* Throne:
> This that *Parmenio*, who still over-came,
> Yet gave his Master the immortall fame;
> Who for his prudence, valour, care, and trust,
> Had this reward most cruel, and unjust. (p. 145)

Throughout the poem, Alexander is acutely conscious of
his mortality and envies Achilles, whom he fancies his ancestor, in having Homer to sing his praises and grant him immortality and lasting fame. It is, therefore, a final irony that
Bradstreet should cite Seneca's castigation of Alexander's
murder of another trusted adviser, Calisthenes (pp. 146–147),
as the conqueror's most lasting literary monument. And she
adds her own observations (possibly echoing Mark Antony in
Shakespeare's *Julius Caesar*):

> His vertues dead, buried, and all forgot,
> But vice remains, to his eternall blot. (p. 143)

Bradstreet's detailed examination of kings and their affairs of state in "Alexander the Great" and "The Four Monarchies" as a whole leads her quite naturally into the "Dialogue Between Old and New England." The two poems represent a juxtaposition of the remote past to the recent past and historical present. As New England summarizes English history, we become aware, if we were not already from a reading of "The Four Monarchies," that there is an essential continuity of bloody experience in lands ruled by kings whose will goes unchecked by a consideration of their subjects' wishes and whose laws are at odds with divine decrees. But Bradstreet's voice is now untinged with irony as she exhorts England to

> . . . sack proud *Rome*, and all her vassalls rout:
> There let thy name, thy fame, thy valour shine,
> As did thine Ancestours in *Palentine*. . . . (p. 189)

The difference between the tone of this poem and the tone of "The Four Monarchies" is the result not only of Bradstreet's fervent nationalism, which she shared with most other New Englanders of her day, but also of her firm belief in the truth of the protestant religion. For the wars against Rome and the Turkish empire which she calls for are Wars of the Lord, not fought for petty and selfish ends as were Alexander's or Xerxes', but for the spread of Christian truth and the Kingdom of God. Divinely approved ends justify the deeds she counsels and, moreover, place the conquests she anticipates outside the province of vanity and time.

Only once in the second grouping of poems does Bradstreet adopt a self-deprecating and submissive feminine voice reminiscent of the tone in the first section of *The Tenth Muse.* Speaking of her decision to abort the projected four monarchies and to deal with only three of them, she writes: "This task [i.e., the writing of historical poetry] befits not Women like to Men" (p. 174). Yet even this observation seems motivated as much by critical awareness that "the Subject was too high, beyond my straine" (p. 174) as by her simple surrender to masculine superiority. Moreover, the Muse triumphs in the end, for Bradstreet does return to her task after several days' respite to begin and complete the fourth monarchy, the Roman kings, though the brevity of her treatment suggests that her reasons for completing the project had more to do with her desire for numerical unity than with poetic inspiration: the Quaternions should be balanced by four monarchies. Whatever her intentions as she wrote her historical survey and her versified discussion of English history and current events, then, the poems register a change from simple acquiescence to the concept of male supremacy in the arts and in politics to a more questioning and critical attitude. For the most part, it is this new point of view, matched with an increased confidence in the worth of her own ideas, that prevails in the third section of the volume.

III

The transition from the historical material of the second section of *The Tenth Muse* to the third and last part, the one comprised of elegies, epitaphs, and a final verse on the vanity of all things, is achieved by means of one swift line at the beginning of the "Elegie upon . . . Sir Philip Sidney": "When England did injoy her Halsion dayes" (p. 191). The mood now is reflective after the tumult of "The Four Monarchies" and "A Dialogue." The theme of England's halcyon days is fully developed in the elegy on Queen Elizabeth, where Bradstreet conjoins it with overt resistance to the doctrine of male supremacy:

Now say, have women worth, or have they none?
Or had they some, but with our Queen is't gone?
Nay Masculines, you have thus tax'd us long,
But she though dead, will vindicate our wrong.
Let such, as say our sex is void of reason,
Know 'tis a slander now, but once was treason. (pp. 202–203)

In this one respect, then, it appears that *The Tenth Muse* has progressed lineally from section one to section three, in which Bradstreet directly challenges the idea that men are uniquely equipped by nature to rule great nations. (She foreshadowed this challenge in her account of Semiramis, the shame and glory of her sex, but did not extend it directly at that time because the Assyrian Queen was hardly the woman to base her claims upon.) In this connection, it seems significant that Bradstreet willingly pits her evaluation of Sidney's poetry against the narrowmindedness of those who object to his sensuality. "He's a beetle head," she asserts, perhaps punning upon the hair style of the Puritans themselves, "that cann't discry/ A world of treasure, in that rubbish lye" (p. 192). She has in all ways become more self assertive, even to the point of arguing that lasting fame may be sufficient immortality for man. Since these elegies were composed earlier than some of the verses that precede them in *The Tenth Muse*, their placement at the end of the volume may be a deliberate piece of literary strategy meant to direct attention to the change in tone and attitude from the first poems to the last. Read in this way, at any rate, *The Tenth Muse* subtly announces the shift from public to private poet, from a writer saying only what is acceptable to one possessed of her own convictions and willing to utter them or to make them the basis for her art. As the dates of composition indicate, Bradstreet had her own ideas as early as 1638, the year of the elegy on Sidney. Perhaps it was the experience of writing those long, tedious "Four Monarchies" that gave her the confidence to turn increasingly toward her own psychological and critical resources for the subject matter of her poetry.[9]

A more conventional elegy than those on Sidney, du Bartas, and Queen Elizabeth is "Davids Lamentation for Saul, and Jonathan," a close paraphrase of 2 Sam. 1:19. The final couplet—"How are the mighty falne in decay,/ And war-like weapons perished away" (p. 205)—looks two ways at once. It is a fitting epitaph for the history of "The Four Mon-

archies," and it provides a transition to the opening couplet of
the next and final poem, "Of the Vanity of All Worldly
Creatures":

> As he said vanity, so vain say I,
> O vanity, O vain all under skie. (p. 206)

Conventional as the language and the sentiments of this
loose paraphrase of Ecclesiastes are, the reader who has paid
attention to Bradstreet's themes throughout acknowledges an
indisputable appropriateness in them. After the deaths of the
great, the gifted, and the noble, as well as of the base, after
the four ages of man on this earth have passed and his sands
are run out, what remains? Only the wisdom that all is vain,
that all life is flux and change and leads finally to death, and
that only Christ promises permanence. The poem nicely (if
unexcitingly) fuses Old Testament insight into the human
condition with New Testament doctrines. And we are reminded by individual lines in the poem itself—

> And wilst they live, how oft doth turn their State?
> He's now a slave, that was a Prince of late.
>
> .   .   .   .
>
> What, Is't [consolation] in flowring youth, or manly age?
> The first is prone to vice, the last to rage (p. 206)—

that this final statement proceeds inexorably from the other
poems in *The Tenth Muse*, as much as or more than from
Bradstreet's religious convictions.[10]

How much of this complexity of *The Tenth Muse* was
Bradstreet herself aware of? At this distance in time, it is probably impossible to answer that question with any degree of
definiteness. But it is no final argument against the possible
deliberateness of the design that the poems were published
without her knowledge, for she had evidently given her father a
complete manuscript and, moreover, John Woodbridge says
nothing about doing any editorial work. The book was prob-

ably printed, then, as she had arranged it for her father's perusal: A Dedication, a Prologue, Four Elements, Four Humours, Four Ages of Man, Four Seasons, Four Monarchies, a Dialogue in which New England speaks four times in response to three comments and an action on the part of Old England, Four Elegies, and an Afterword. The careful attention Bradstreet paid to the structure of her book ought to be immediately evident to anyone who considers this patterned arrangement.

Even more significant than this organizational plan is the evidence that Bradstreet was willing to disturb the numerical neatness of the whole in her design to add more poems to a second edition of *The Tenth Muse*. Into the final section she wished to incorporate two elegies, one on her father and one on her mother, "Contemplations," "The Flesh and the Spirit," and "The Author to Her Book." The two elegies on her parents obviously belong with the other elegiac verses, and it seems just as obvious that "Contemplations," an extended meditation on time and decay,[11] and "The Flesh and the Spirit," also a poem which contrasts mortal things with immortal essences, belong before "Of the Vanity of All Worldly Creatures" and after the elegies. Whatever the actual circumstances of their composition, in the context of the revised *Tenth Muse* they suggest contemplations arising out of the entire book of poems which precedes them. They intensify our awareness of the themes of flux and change that preoccupied Anne Bradstreet as they did many of her contemporaries, and they indicate that her quest for permanence and stability found at least partial expression in her concern for the unity of her book. Only "The Author to Her Book" appears to disturb that unity, and even in this case, one suspects, the heightened critical consciousness which the poem reflects owes something to her idea that powerfully formed rhymes may, in the end, outlast all the marble monuments of princes.[12]

On the other hand, Bradstreet's dogged persistence to finish

"The Four Monarchies," an event happily prevented by the
fire which destroyed the Bradstreet home and her manuscript
in 1666, testifies that she did not understand the ironic circularity of the poem she had created to that point. This is no
sure evidence, however, that she would not have concluded it
with a similar irony—perhaps with Parliament advising and,
in large measure, curbing the excesses of kings, as she ended the
"Dialogue." In light of these textual uncertainties, it seems best
to close with caution. The unity of *The Tenth Muse* appears
to be the result both of careful planning, as the numerical
design indicates, and of the author's preoccupation with a
single theme. Its developing feminine voice may well be the
work of accident, but there are some reasons for believing, as
I have suggested, that Anne Bradstreet may have been at least
partially aware of that element of her book. While *The Tenth
Muse* is not likely to become as popular among students of
American literature as her later, more lyrical poetry, then, it
nevertheless amply rewards close reading. There is no reason
for us to feel in the future as embarrassedly apologetic about
the book as we have become used to feeling in the past.

ROBERT D. ARNER

UNIVERSITY OF CINCINNATI

Notes

1. The studies to which I refer include Josephine Ketcham Piercy's
Anne Bradstreet (New York: Twayne, 1965); Elizabeth Wade White's
Anne Bradstreet: "The Tenth Muse" (New York: Oxford Univ. Press,
1971); White's "The Tenth Muse—A Tercentenary Appraisal of Anne
Bradstreet," *William and Mary Quarterly* 7 (1951): 353–77; Ann Stanford's
"Anne Bradstreet; Dogmatist and Rebel," *New England Quarterly* 39
(1966): 373–89; Rosemary M. Laughlin's "Anne Bradstreet: Poet in Search
of Form," *American Literature* 42 (1970): 1–17; and Alvin Rosenfeld's
"Anne Bradstreet's 'Contemplations': Patterns of Form and Meaning," *New
England Quarterly* 43 (1970): 79–96.

White's book I find both rewarding for its wealth of biographical information and unsatisfactory for its criticism. So far as this paper is concerned,
I take issue with her claim that "there is both chronological and textual

confusion in the order in which these poems [in *The Tenth Muse*] were printed" and question the absoluteness of her assertion that Bradstreet would have rearranged them if she had been able to supervise the publication of her 1650 edition (pp. 253–54). As I attempt to argue in this essay, the structure of the book as it now exists shows considerable imagination on Mistress Bradstreet's part and even reflects a development in her attitudes toward woman's role in society, whether the poet was herself fully aware of that development or not. Further, nearly all the good poems in the volume stand at the end in its present arrangement and thus suggest the writer's own evaluation of her work and her sense of her poems' merits, whereas the chronological pattern proposed by White lacks both imagination and internal rationale.

2. Samuel Eliot Morison, *Builders of the Bay Colony* (1930; rpt. Boston: Houghton Mifflin, 1958), p. 330.

3. For this and all other quotations from *The Tenth Muse*, the text is Josephine Piercy's facsimile edition (Gainesville, Fla.: Scholars' Facsimiles & Reprints, 1965). Woodbridge's comment appears on A3, verso. Passages from Bradstreet's poems will be indicated in the text according to their pagination in this edition.

4. See White's *Anne Bradstreet*, pp. 246–48, for the interesting hypothesis that in "David's Lamentation for Saul and Jonathan" Bradstreet may have been using a biblical passage to comment upon current political events, the execution of Charles I, much in the manner of Dryden's *Absalom and Achitophel*. If this is so, then the likelihood that more than history is involved in Bradstreet's historical survey of the four monarchies increases.

5. Stanford, 379.

6. Laughlin, 15, notes: "It can be observed that Bradstreet was constantly questing for unity, unity in matter and spirit." This quest, we might add, can probably be traced to her acute awareness of time, change, and impermanence.

7. See Austin Warren, "Edward Taylor's Poetry: Colonial Baroque," *Kenyon Review* 3 (1941): 355–71.

8. Bradstreet's view of history was probably conditioned by her reading of Raleigh, who noted in his *The History of the World. . . :*

For who hath not observed, what labour, practice peril, bloodshed, and cruelty, the Kings and Princes of the World have undergone, exercised, taken on them, and committed; to make themselves and their Issues Masters of the World? And yet hath Babylon, Persia, Egypt, Syria, Macedon, Carthage, Rome, and the rest, no fruit, no flower, grass, nor leaf, springing upon the face of the earth, of those seeds: No, their very roots and ruines do hardly remain.

9. See both Stanford (378–79) and White (360–61) for additional comments on the psychological significance of the elegies and "The Four Monarchies" for Bradstreet.

10. "Meditations 52" of "Meditations Divine and Moral" confirms the hypothesis that personal experience and observation were sources of Bradstreet's philosophy of vanity equally as important as *Ecclesiastes*. She writes:

> Had not the wisest of men taught us this lesson that all is vanity and vexation of spirit, yet our own experience would soon have spelled it out, for what do we obtain of all these things, but it is with labour and vexation? When we enjoy them it is vanity and vexation, and if we loose [*sic*] them, then they are less than vanity and more than vexation, so that we have good cause often to repeat that sentence: vanity of vanities, vanity of vanities, all is vanity.

The Works of Anne Bradstreet, ed. Jeannine Hensley (Cambridge, Mass.: Harvard Univ. Press, 1967), p. 283.

11. Rosenfeld discusses this theme in "Contemplations" in terms of the fusion of the "graved white stone image" in Stanza 33 of *Revelation* and Shakespeare's Sonnet LV: "Not marble, nor the gilded monuments/Of princes. . . ."

12. Again, see Rosenfeld's discussion of this idea, esp. pp. 90–96. According to my reading of "The Author to Her Book," this final poem in the *Several Poems* (1678) edition would leave us with a last counterstatement to "Of the Vanity of All Worldly Creatures." Thus the structure of the revised text reflects the unresolved tension between doctrine and private feeling that we find especially prominent in Bradstreet's later poems, particularly in the lyrical poems addressed to her husband.

EDWARD TAYLOR'S

"A FIG FOR THEE OH! DEATH"

Sometime in the early 1720s, Edward Taylor, believing that his death was near, wrote "A Fig for thee Oh! Death," a poem in the *ars moriendi* tradition.[1] The similarities between this poem and the perennially popular manual on dying, Edward Pearse's *The Great Concern, or A Serious Warning for a Timely and Thorough Preparation for Death*, suggest that Taylor referred to Pearse during the composition of the poem.[2] Pearse, however, was only a starting point; Taylor's lifelong apprenticeship in his craft enabled him to adapt traditional material to produce the poetic vision which summarizes his attitude toward death and salvation.

Taylor's poem and Pearse's manual for dying originate in parallel situations. Despite the fact that Taylor had recovered from his illness of December 1720, he knew he was fast approaching the answer to an old problem—the question of his salvation. Taylor was so sure that he would soon appear before "Christ's bright face" that he steeled himself to relinquish all earthly concerns:

My House & lands, my Stock & State I finde
Can't ease my tooth's nor Head ach nor my minde:

My Friends & mine acquaintances very deare,
My Deare-Deare Wife & little twigs that peare
Out of my Stock, Bits of myself, I finde
Exceeding dear whom now I leave behinde.[3]

Edward Pearse wrote his book under similar conditions. "God has kept me for full half a year by the Gracious side while lifting me up, then calling me down, and now he seems to be speedily finishing my days." Having suffered a lengthy illness, Pearse pens his farewell to the "World . . . Friends and Relations . . . Eating and Drinking . . . Sin and Sinning," and prepares to be with his Lord.[4]

Various minor images also suggest parallels between the two works. Taylor employs a series of container images when referring to his body and the grave: "Cask," and "Cave," "Mill," and "Van." The "Trap Door of Hell" initiates the series. Significantly, Edward Pearse connects the stage, or door to death, for his Puritan audience. Interpreting Psalm 39:13, he says that David's meaning is that "if God did not go on to afflict him, as he had done, he must sudddenly die, suddenly go off the Stage of this World, and go down to the Bars of death, to the gates of the Grave" (p. 5). Another series of images concerns the effects of death upon the Body and Soul, particularly the physical change that occurs at death. The Body must die for the Soul to be reborn, and Taylor's soul agrees by refusing to fight ". . . For this my Flesh" (line 24). The body must become food for worms, Death's "Mess." In his discussion of the dissolution between Body and Soul, Pearse uses this same striking image of the Body as death's mess; Death "turns a living Body into a dead Carcass, a lifeless lump of Clay, and causeth it to become meat for worms to feed on" (p. 4).

Not all changes caused by death are physical, nor are they visible. Traditionally, the Christian has three enemies—the Flesh, the Devil, and the World—all three of which must be

overcome before the Soul can reach its spiritual home. According to the movement of the images in the first part of "A Fig
for thee," the Flesh must be eaten by worms and thus defeated, before the Soul can rise to Glory. It is at this time
that a great battle commences between the Soul and its two
remaining enemies—the Devil and the World:

> I am resolvde to fight thee, and ne'er yield
> Blood up to th' Ears; and in the battle field
> Chasing thee hence: But not for this my Flesh . . .
>
> (lines 21–24).

In chapter 2 Pearse notes that it is in the dying hour that
". . . the Devil is most fierce and terrible in his assaults and
Temptations upon the Soul . . . and now the Battel [for
the Soul] is to be won or lost forever; therefore now he roars
and rages terribly indeed, discharges all his Murdering Pieces
against the Soul" (pp. 10–11). The Devil is most fierce, he
says, first,

> when a man is going from Sin to Grace, when he is fully re-
> solved to choose with Christ, to shake off the Yoke of Sin, and
> to take upon him the Yoke of Jesus. The Second is, When a
> man is going from Sin to Grace; when he is going off the Stage
> of Time to Eternity; when a Man begins to live a Spiritual Life,
> and when a Man comes to die a Natural Death (p. 11).

Although these minor images—found often in other Puritan
devotional works—establish a general correspondence between
the book and the poem, it is in the image of the "King of
Terrours" that Taylor's indebtedness to *The Great Concern*
seems most evident. In chapters 2 and 3, Pearse focuses upon
the image: "Indeed 'tis therefore called the King of Terrours,
because it is the greatest and strongest Terror. And Death
must needs be Terrible in it self" (p. 7). In the next reference,
however, Pearse insists on the Soul's triumph over death: "But
now take a Soul that has all things right and in order for his

Spiritual Concerns, and he is carried above the fear of this King of Terrors" (p. 23). Not only does Taylor begin his poem with this specific image, "Thou King of Terrours with Thy Gastly Eyes," and allude to it throughout the poem ("Thy Gastly Face," "Why / Then should this grimace at me terrify"), but the image provides the poet the focal point he needs to initiate his poetic vision that will move beyond Death to the King of Glory. Taylor's poem, in fact, closely follows Pearse's advice to the meditator.

In the latter part of *The Great Concern*, Pearse presents specific directions about preparation for death. He tells the reader to remember the coming "Days of Darkness." To ready the Soul, one must "be much and frequent in the Contemplation of Death and the Grave . . . ; therefore walk among the Tombs, and converse much and frequently with the Thoughts of a dying hour" (pp. 70–71). The contemplation of the Death's Head is a frequent theme of *memento mori* poetry, and Taylor's first line is also a reflection of the Death's image, ". . . With Butter teeth." He envisions the Death's Head on the Puritan tombstone, with its square, extended teeth.[5] The imagined symbol of man's mortality with its hollow, staring eye-holes, provides the dramatic context of the poem. Taylor speaks directly to the symbol of death, creating a monologue that reaffirms his belief in Christ's victory over death. Of course, the King of Terrors is also a biblical image referring specifically to Job's facing Satan: "His confidence shall be rooted out of his tabernacle, and it shall bring him to the King of Terrors" (Job 18:14).[6]

Pearse and Taylor also reflect a common use of precise biblical passages. Isaiah 34 and 35, for example, have traditionally been read as an oracle of judgment and a prophecy of salvation. Chapter 34 contains a description of God's judgment of the nations, a judgment which takes place in the bloody battlefield of this world. Pearse makes extensive use of the *Acel-*

dama or Field of Blood to explain why the believer should not covet the World:

> It is an angry World, a frowning, a dirty, a bewitching World: 'Tis a waste, howling Wilderness, a strange Land, an Hour of Bondage, a troublesome tempestuous Sea, an Aceldama, a Field of Blood (p. 75).

His references parallel Taylor's powerful condemnation of the World in lines 21–22: "I am resolvde to fight thee, and ne'er yield, / Blood up to th' Ears. . . ." The biblical passages of Isaiah 34 also contain numerous references to blood as a symbol of God's judgment. The prophet sees the mountains melted with the blood of the dead; God's sword will be bathed in heaven: "The sword of the Lord is filled with blood . . . and with the blood of lambs and goats." The images conclude in verse seven, which coincides with Taylor's poetic vision: "and their land shall be soaked with blood . . ." (Isaiah 34:3–7). Pearse also reveals the Field of Blood as the scene of Judgment:

> Death when ever it comes, will turn your Conflicts into Victory; this Aceldama or Field of Blood (for such is the World) will turn your conflicts into a Mount of Triumph, and a Throne of Glory. What is this World but an Aceldama, a Field of Blood, to the poor saints? (p. 160).

Finally, Taylor's resolve to fight occurs at the moment he faces death; this becomes the dominant period of time in the second section of the poem. In the same way, the prophet stresses the immediate presentness of death and judgment and carries it throughout his statements, from the exordium of verse one ("Come near, ye nations to hear"), to the picture of blood in verse six ("the sword of the Lord is filled with blood"), to the Judgment itself in verse eight ("for it is the day of the Lord's vengeance, and the year of recompences for the controversy of Zion").

The Great Concern, with its use of similar image patterns, is a source, then, which Taylor no doubt had in mind while writing "A Fig for thee." Taylor rediscovered in Pearse's work biblical image patterns (particularly the King of Terrours) which in part prompted the poem. Beyond these basic parallels, however, Taylor creates a complex poetic vision. The simplest and most obvious aspects of the poem are the structure of the dramatic monologue and the image of the Death's Head on the stone in the graveyard scene; both are combined in three sections, each one of which moves from death to salvation. The first section (lines 1–20) progresses from the image of Death to Taylor's assurance of Grace. The "King of Terrours" becomes "not so frightful now to me" and the "Gastly face / . . . not so dreadfull unto mee through Grace" (19–20). The same is true of the second unit of the poem (21–50). The direct address to Death appears in the first line of this section, "I am resolvde to fight thee" (21), and moves toward the poet's desire to be part of the General Resurrection where "The Soule and Body now, as two true Lovers / Ery night . . . do hug and kiss each other" (47–48). Section three (52–56) completes the cycle. Taylor shifts momentarily to the death's head with its terrifying "grimace" (52), but he ends triumphantly, assured of salvation and contemptuous of death: "I still am where I was, a Fig for thee" (56). Thus, while the poem is divided into several segments moving from death to salvation, the idea of the graveyard unites all parts. Taylor begins with the lengthy description of tombstone and grave in the first six lines, alludes often to the figure, and returns to a single reminder of the dramatic situation in the third section, "why / Then should this grimace at me terrify?".

To this dramatic context, Taylor incorporates the allegorical pattern of Body and Soul as lovers dissolved by death and reunited at the Resurrection, developing images not found in Pearse nor in the biblical texts, which provide the underlying imagistic structure of the poem. The allegorical form of the *descriptio mortis* of lines 11 to 18 is fairly standard.[7] There is nothing unusual in presenting the Body as the "shell" or "kir-nells box" and the Soul as the 'kirnell," the "nut," which the worms (Sin) eat before it ascends.[8] Even Taylor's image of the transformation which the Soul undergoes between the time when it is consumed by the worms and the moment it is carried to heaven on angel's wings remains traditional.[9] Each body and soul will be "raised up anew and made all bright / and Christalized," made members of the Mystical Body. Like the butterfly in its final stages in the cocoon, the Soul shall be truly cleansed, as clear and transparent as "crystal," free of corruptible bonds. Death brings rebirth, but in a newer, purer form which the Soul assumes when "Christalized."

Taylor's distinctive imagery, however, appears in the description of Body and Soul in the second section of the poem.[10] Had he presented the traditional battleground for the Soul's fight against Satan, the setting would have been Hell, the battle being akin to Christ's harrowing of Hell to save Adam and his kind. But Taylor has no harrowing of Hell; his emphasis places the World as the battleground, and his Soul, although closely aligned with the figure of Christ Militant coming to do battle, is not attacking the Body; for the Soul already sees "her" as evil ("Labouring to drown me into Sin"), which accounts for Taylor's presenting the Body as "my vile harlot" and "my strumpet." Instead of the conventional war between Body and Soul, Taylor places the major conflict between the Soul and Death.

Death becomes the Soul's opponent, who will rape the Body unless the Soul restrains him. Death must take "her captive," imprison her in his "dungeon Cave," the grave, and perform the rape ("and grinde to powder in thy Mill, the grave"). The images in the battle between the Soul and Death are thus extended because of the sexual imagery. Some are explicit, such as "my vile harlot" and "my strumpet," and they help establish the context from which less obvious sexual references emerge. One passage is an excellent example of Taylor's use of multi-level imagery:

> Labouring to drown me into Sin, disguise
> By Eating and by drinking such evill joyes
> Though Grace preserv'd mee that I nere have
> Surprised been nor tumbled in such grave.
> Hence for my strumpet I'le ne'er draw my Sword . . .
>
> (lines 25–29).

Taken in the context of the "strumpet" image, the basic structure of the imagery in this passage is a clear example of Taylor's word-play, the lady or the Body being the Covenant of Works which the Soul rejects in favor of the Covenant of Grace and Salvation. Taylor's "sword" is, of course, Isaiah's wet and bloody sword of God, come for the Body's judgment; it is also the Soul's refusal to defend the Body; and in its phallic connotations, it is Taylor's refusal to be trapped by the Carnal World. The same is true for "tumbled in such grave." Through the pun Taylor refers to the opposing covenants: Grace has preserved the Soul from "tumbling-in-such-grave" error as depending upon good works; [11] it is, moreover, the Soul's reward when it is reborn on the wings of the angel instead of being placed in Death's mill; and, finally, it indicates that the Soul will be cleansed without being raped or defiled by death or the grave.

The sexual imagery, in fact, connects all parts of the poem and becomes, with the dramatic structure, a major unifying factor. Consider, for example, lines 32–37:

> But let thy frozen gripes take her Captive
> And her imprison in thy dungeon Cave
> And grinde to powder in thy Mill the grave,
> Which powder in thy Van thou'st safely keep
> Till she hath slept out quite her fatall Sleep.
> When the last Cock shall Crow the last day in. . . .

In most basic terms, the meaning is consistent with Christian doctrine—the Body must die and be placed in the grave to await Gabriel's call on the day when the saints will be made whole. But the extension of the meaning follows consistently Taylor's earlier passages. "Frozen gripes" is reminiscent of the King of Terrours with "Grizzly Hide and clawing Tallons." "Dungeon Cave," "Van," and particularly "Mill the grave" correspond to the "Trap Door of Hell," since they are part of the container and grinding images focusing on the grave itself. The connection is continued with "her fatall Sleep," as Taylor develops the Body's sleep and rising around the Alba, the parting of lovers at the break of day. Dawn, when satisfied lovers normally would part, becomes for Taylor the General Resurrection when worldly lovers will separate, but the "true lovers" will be reunited in heaven. The grinding image is another important sexual reference—viewed in terms of a woman (Body) being abducted by a rapist (Death) and carried to the dungeon cave, the meaning becomes obvious. Similar to the motion of grinding is the pounding of the Flesh by the Poundrill. The same is true of the "knocks," "blows," and "cracks" of Death on the body in Death's attack. Both the Poundrill and Death's attack foreshadow the more explicit sexual terms that appear in Section Two, and they take on new meaning once the sexual images appear. With the mention of the Mill, grinding is linked to another image, the "powder" and "dust" which will appear in "Death's smoky furnace." These images show another stage of bodily disintegration within the grave, thus continuing the action established by the "Poundrill." They also anticipate the time when the Soul will be "Christalized," "refinde," the pure condition the Body must assume before it "entertains its Soule again in bliss." The focal point for the cycle of death to eternal life is the love affair between the Body and Soul, and the sexual images allow Taylor to create a strikingly complex interrelationship of images.

Taylor's final line, "I still am where I was, a Fig for thee," through the image of the fig, unites the previous levels of imagery. Assured of his Soul's peace, Taylor denounces Death by making the *Fica*, contemptuously thrusting his thumb between two of his closed fingers. The "fig" is his sign of contempt. Convinced of ultimate victory over death, Taylor knows that although all material goods must pass away, he shall be with God and the saints even after the Lord's destruction of the physical universe. Thus God's judgment of Taylor is a judgment of the Puritan nation and all saints who have preceded him. In Isaiah 34, the prophet moves from personal to cosmic judgment; he speaks of destruction upon the nations and armies (v. 2), and a cosmic levelling of the world (v. 4). The stars, or hosts of heaven, will be dissolved, with the heavens rolled up as a scroll. When this occurs, "all their host [stars] shall fall down, as the leaf falleth off from the vine, and as a falling fig from the fig tree." Taylor employs the same cosmic dimensions for his poem, by covering the three most significant Christian events—the Fall, the Crucifixion, and the Resurrection—and by shifting his point of view from personal death to general salvation. From the singular view that death is "not so frightfull now to me," he moves to the last day when God shall seek "all there round." Thus Taylor raises his poem from a death manual on a specific occasion to a portrayal of the Last Judgment and the Resurrection on a cosmic scale, with the fig, an Old Testament symbol of both peace and judgment, becoming the sign of Taylor's movement beyond death to salvation.[12] Micah declares that when war ends "then shall sit every man under his vine and fig tree" (4:4); Isaiah shows that the sign of judgment is the "falling fig" (34:4); and both prophecies will be fulfilled when God opens "the sixth seal": the stars of heaven will fall to earth, "even as a fig tree casteth her untimely figs" (Rev. 6:12–14). And the Puritan saints, including Edward Taylor will be brought to judgment and salvation. Death may have the Body, the fig, but to the Lord belongs Taylor's Soul.

ARTHUR FORSTATER

THOMAS M. DAVIS

KENT STATE UNIVERSITY

"A Fig for thee Oh! Death" [Manuscript Book Version]

Thou King of Terrours with thy Gastly Eyes,
With Butter teeth, bare bones Looks frighting guise.
With grim, & Grizzly hide & claws as fell
That fang & tare, the black trapdoors of Hell.
5 To all impenitents that on do trip,
In Sinfull plight to the infernall pit.
Thou dasht thy Venom Tush on my Lord's side,
Who struck it out, & all its poison 'stroyde.
That now thy Poundrill doth onely pound
10 My Caske to pieces, stowing under ground.
Thou'rt not so terrible to me nor thy knocks
My heavenly Sparke's kept up in its screw box.
It is most Safe, thou onely brakst its Shell,
Thy teeth its Nut cracks: its Kernells Well.
15 Its pickt out fair & bright & so by worms
Not Viciated but most shining turns,
Leaps on an Angell back, on which it flies
Up to Christ, brightest glory of best joyes.

2 *guise*] conj. 11 *terrible*] conj. 12 *Sparke's*] Sparkes *box.*] box 13
Shell,] Shell 14 *Well.*] Well 15 *& so by worms*] orig: & not by worms
16 *turns,* turns 18 *Christ,*] Christ *of best joyes*] orig: *of best of joyes* 20
Hooks.] conj.

Hence thou to mee with all thy Ghostly Looks
20 Bearst not such dread within thy rending Hooks.
I am resolv'd to fight thee, and not yield,
Blood up to th' eares, here in the battlefield.
And Chase thee thence, yet not for this my flesh,
My harlot body, make thou it thy Mess,
25 That oft ensnared mee with its Strumpets guise
Of Meats & drinks dainty Sensualities.
Yet Grace ne'er suffer me to turn aside
As Sinners oft in Falling, & do abide.
Hence for this Harlot Ile draw out no sword,
30 Against thee nor add to thy Jaws a Curb,
Nor for its Safty 'gainst thee ever Strive
But leave it to thy frozen fist Captive.
It to imprison in thy dungeon Cave,
And grind to powder in thy Mill the grave,
35 Whose dust thou in thy Vein shall safely keep
Enchested up till it hath slept its sleep.
When the last Cock shall Crow the last day in
And the Arch-Angells Trumpet loud shall ring:
When the Omniscient Eye shall finde all round
40 Each dust Death's mill had very findly ground
Which in death's Chymick Furnace's all refinde
And Each to 'ts fellow most exactly joyn'd
And up araised a New fabrick bright
Cleare Chrystalized, top full of delight,
45 To entertain the Spirits, Soul in bliss,
The holy Angells waiting then on this,
Bringing the Soul & body as true Lovers
Together hand in heart unto Each others.
Which at their meeting ravished with joyes
50 How do they hug & Kiss each other's Eyes?
And hand in hand ascending up on high
Into Eternall glory gloriously?
Is this the Worst thou king of terrours? Why

Then should thy terrors ere me terrify?
55 Why comst so softly on, amend thy pace,
Thy Slowness me delays from Christs blesst face.
All tho' thou art drest up in terrours to fright mee,
I dread thee nott, & say, a Fig for thee.

22 *battlefield.*] battlefield   26 *Sensualities.*] Sensualities   30 *add*] conj.   35
Vein] Ven   40 *Death's*] Death   41 *death's*] death
42 *to 'ts*] to 't   50 *other's*] other   51 *ascending up on high*] orig: ascend
on high

Notes

1. *The Poems of Edward Taylor,* ed. Donald E. Stanford (New Haven,
Conn.: Yale Univ. Press, 1960), pp. 486–89. An earlier version of the poem
(see Appendix) exists in Taylor's "Manuscript Book" (see Stanford, Item 3,
p. 507) in the Yale University Library, to whom we are indebted for
permission to publish this version.

"A Fig for thee" was probably written after Taylor's recovery from a
serious illness in December of 1720; a number of poems on similar themes
were written at this time. See Thomas M. Davis, "Edward Taylor's 'Valedictory' Poems," *Early American Literature* 7 (Spring 1972), particularly
the introductory comments.

2. Taylor owned a copy of Pearse's volume; see *The Poetical Works of
Edward Taylor,* ed. Thomas H. Johnson (Princeton, N.J.: Princeton Univ.
Press, 1939), Item 144, p. 216. *The Great Concern* had appeared in 25 edi-
tions by 1715. For an analysis of Calvinistic attitudes toward the prepara-
tion for death, see Nancy Beatty, *The Craft of Dying* (New Haven, Conn.:
Yale Univ. Press, 1970), particularly chap. 3.

3. "Valedictory Poems," p. 46.

4. *The Great Concern* (Boston, 1711), p. A2. Subsequent page references
refer to this edition, the 22d.

5. Taylor uses the "King of Terrours" as a composite visual image of the
Death's Head, derived from its use in New England tombstone carving,
emblem books, and broadsides. See Allen I. Ludwig, *Graven Images: New
England Stone Carving and Its Symbols, 1650–1815* (Middletown, Conn.:
Wesleyan Univ. Press, 1966), Plates 10a and 10b; Ola Elizabeth Winslow,
American Broadside Verse . . . (New Haven, Conn.: Yale Univ. Press,
1930), p. 27; Rosemary Freeman, *English Emblem Books* (London, 1970),
p. 25. See also Taylor's use of the same image in *Meditations* 1: 34 and
2: 112.

6. There are, of course, other parallels between the two works. Even
Taylor's "Iron Curb," which he had used in "God's Determinations touch-

ing his Elect" (p. 415), is similar to Pearse's discussion of the Devil's role at the moment of death. In order to prevent Satan from turning accuser, from charging the Soul with its sins, and from attacking the soul as a hypocrite, "God can and sometimes does chain him up, so that he shall not be able to trouble and torment the Saints in their passage out of this World." Also present in both is the idea of Body and Soul as lovers; Pearse, however, does not focus on the explicit sexual imagery that dominates the poem. Pearse's strongest statement appears in chapter 2: "Death is indeed the rending of Body and Soul, (those old and loving Companions) asunder" (p. 8).

7. One difference between the "Manuscript book" version and the final copy, besides the two additional lines in the former, is the appearance of the Screw Box image within the *descriptio mortis*. No doubt, it is part of the enclosure images, as are "thy vein" and "enchested up" of lines 35–36.

8. For a discussion of the widespread use of such imagery, see Elizabeth Wiley, "Sources of Imagery in the Poetry of Edward Taylor" (Ph.D. diss., Univ. of Pittsburgh, 1962), pp. 119–20.

9. See Dionysus of Fourna, *Christian Iconography*, ed. Adolphe Didron (New York: B. Franklin, 1968), 2: 175–76 (fig. 213).

10. This section contains the additional couplet which Taylor deleted in the final version:

Which at their meeting ravished with joyes
How do they hug & Kiss each other's Eyes? (lines 49–50).

11. It is the use of such complex word play which suggests that the "Manuscript Book" version is the earlier working copy from which Taylor produced the final version of "A Fig for thee Oh! Death." Taylor's belief that when the General Resurrection occurs bodies will be made whole, lost limbs connected to sockets, is carried through the phrase "Each to'ts fellow hath exactly joyn't"; and the line demonstrates his more precise use of language in the final copy. Images such as the "screw box" and "Chymick Furnace's" have been deleted while others such as the "kirnells will" or "curb" have been sharpened for emphasis to "Heavenly kirnells box" and "Iron Curb." The wordiness of the first copy and the strained lines and rhymes ("Nor for its Safty 'gainst thee ever strive / But leave it to thy Frozen fist Captive") have been eliminated.

12. For additional biblical uses of the fig as a symbol of peace see 1 Kings 4:25, 2 Kings 18:31, Joel 2:22, Zechariah 3:10.

II.

COPLEY'S *WATSON AND THE SHARK*

AND AESTHETICS IN THE 1770s

"The war has begun," wrote John Singleton Copley to his wife on 2 July 1776, "and, if I am not mistaken, the country, which was once the happiest on the globe, will be deluged with blood for many years." [1] The enormous fact of the political revolution of the last third of the eighteenth century has for a long time been allowed to define the aesthetic character of the age, and with some justification; but the understanding of the quality of American aesthetic life has also suffered thereby, for numerous issues were only tangentially touched by the political change. If the period is, as it has so often been called, an age of transition between colonial patterns of aesthetic order and the full flood of romanticism which would give a lasting impress to American art of the nineteenth century and beyond, still it needs to be understood in its own terms, and neither as merely a function of political change nor as a form of belated neoclassicism or as preromanticism. One searches in vain for a neat label which can characterize a period which produced both the lean witty play of Franklin's *Autobiography* and the lush extravagances of Susanna Rowson's *Charlotte Temple* or Brockden Brown's *Wieland*, both the controlled sedateness and intellectual clarity of the Decla-

ration of Independence or Washington's Farewell Address
and the pomposities of Barlow's *Columbiad*, both the lurid
sublimities of Freneau's "House of Night" and the Gold-
smithian pastoralism of his "American Village."

"This is an age of experiments," proclaimed Jeremy Belknap
in 1781,[2] and he, like Franklin, Royall Tyler, Freneau and a
host of others recognized that the new inductive method applied not only to politics or to economic and cultural life
generally, but to aesthetic form as well, to the shaping of
imaginative constructs out of the wide range of choices open
to them as late eighteenth-century American artists. As the
great American political experiment turned from words to
arms in 1775, Copley was already one year an exile, removed
both in space and historic time, copying a Correggio in Parma.
As events turned out, his expatriation would prove to be per-
manent and America's greatest colonial painter would become
an important member of the British artistic community during
his remaining forty years.

The break in Copley's career and its significance must not
be exaggerated, however. Students of American culture have
too much experience with artistic expatriation to equate spatial
removal with loss of American identity. A specific national
consciousness was just in the process of formation during these
years, and European commentators—Paine, Burke, Crevecoeur come immediately to mind—as well as native Americans participated in that transatlantic process of self-definition.
Besides, in 1775 Copley was in his late thirties, with some
twenty years of practice in his craft behind him, and if he
was seeking to experiment in new ways in Europe, he was
by no means trying to deny what he had learned and absorbed
in Boston.

The evidence of this would come some three years later.
Copley was approached by Brook Watson, a prominent London merchant, to do a painting commemorating the incident
in Watson's youth when he had lost his leg and nearly his

life to a shark while swimming in Havana harbor. Copley accepted the challenge of the commission, and the result, exhibited in 1778 at the Royal Academy, was *Watson and the Shark*, one of Copley's masterpieces (Figure 1), and generally acknowledged by art historians to be an important moment not only in the history of Copley and American art, as both emerged from a long apprenticeship in the craft tradition, but also in the aesthetic sensibility of the Western tradition more broadly considered, a landmark which looks at once both back to seventeenth-century baroque precedents and forward to some of the great romantic achievements of the nineteenth century.

The significance of *Watson and the Shark* is finally neither retrospective nor anticipatory but of its own time and place: the moment of 1778 for the expatriate American artist. In fact, the *Watson* is a kind of paradigm of the strengths and weaknesses, the possibilities and problems of American aesthetic achievement at just that moment when American political identity was taking shape through the violence of war. As such it demands the attention not only of the art historian but of all who seek to understand the dynamics of American aesthetic thought and practice during the formative years.

To say this is not to claim for the *Watson* any narrowly nationalistic significance, for the obvious evidence is clearly against that. Copley's patron and subject, Brook Watson, was an Englishman, possibly a Tory agent at the outset of the war, a wealthy merchant who was later to be Lord Mayor of London for a year. The setting of the pictorial anecdote, though New World, was the Spanish harbor of Havana and not the English colonies now struggling for independence. Copley's larger audience for the canvas was English and the voices to which he was most responsive as the canvas took shape were spokesmen for English neoclassical officialdom: the Royal Academy, its president the great Sir Joshua Reynolds, and Copley's sponsor and rival fellow-expatriate, Ben-

jamin West. If West's American political loyalties were clear, despite his royal patronage, Copley's seem to have been intentionally obscure, and even after the war he never returned to the United States.[3]

One must insist upon the relevance of Copley's *Watson and the Shark* to the American aesthetic situation nevertheless, because into that work was filtered all that Copley had brought with him from America and all that he was learning, consciously and unconsciously, about the range of the artist's choices in shaping a work of the imagination. Some of these choices were personal, but in a variety of ways most of them involved questions with which most American artists—in words as well as paint—were struggling during these years. Because Copley's response was particularly powerful, *Watson and the Shark* can offer us some of the larger insights and perspectives we need to come to terms with this aesthetically problematic era.

I. The Pictorial Experience

A study of the significance of *Watson and the Shark* must begin with the impact of the work itself. For most viewers, the visual experience of this large canvas probably begins with a gross apprehension of the highlighted foreground: the eerie figure of the young Watson, the highlighted nose of the shark, the strong whites of the two figures in the boat reaching out towards Watson. The center of the dramatic situation lies here in these three elements, all projected forward towards the picture plane and the viewer, spatially and dramatically interrelated yet separate, gesturing towards one another yet never quite touching, tense and unresolved. We look further, seeking resolution and explanation, release from the tension

Fig. 1. John Singleton Copley. *Watson and the Shark*. 1778. oil on canvas. 71¾ x 90½ inches. National Gallery of Art, Washington, D.C. Ferdinand Lammot Belin Fund.

which, because it is shoved close to us, threatens as it excites and entices. The eye moves through the various figures in the boat and their relation to the event, catches the elegant two-thirds view of the British ship at anchor in the upper left, and eventually explores the background harborscape in its relation to the immediate world of the foreground.

What gradually emerges is a sense of the three worlds of the canvas. The first and most immediate is that of the picture's title subjects, Watson and the shark, each emerging out of the water: Watson, with a kind of unearthly hue that allows us to peer down into the water and almost—but not quite —to see the right foot which the shark has ripped off in his last pass; the shark's head, emerging from the murky darkness of the water on his side in a way that forbids the eye to understand. Neither image is realistic; their value is surreal, iconic, the pure terror of the shark's maw emerging out of darkness, the helplessly beautiful translucency of the Watson figure as much a nightmare image as its counterpart, each emerging from and visually merging into that sea which laps at the edge of the canvas and threatens to spill over onto the viewer.

We are witnesses—indeed, we are made participants in the aesthetic experience of the Burkean Sublime, as the late eighteenth century had come to understand it. The London *General Advertiser*'s reviewer of the Royal Academy exhibition understood this immediately in his comments on the Copley painting:

> He has improved upon the horror of the shark, by leaving it unfinished, and we think he studied narrowly the human mind in this circumstance. No certain and known danger can so powerfully arouse us as when uncertain and unlimited. He gives the mind an idea, and leaves it to conceive its extent.

The impact of the Sublime, by contrast to the order, clarity, harmony of the Beautiful, lay precisely in its indefiniteness, its obscurity, its awesome overwhelming power which involved the viewer while still allowing for a certain aesthetic distance. Burkean aesthetics required the action of the perceiving mind to complete the process, (and herein lay its boldness) made the aesthetic act a psychological process, not merely the passive recognition of qualities inherent in the world "out there." [4]

This is made doubly clear to the viewer because the insecurity we experience in the foreground is opposed to the clarities of Havana harbor, which parade across the upper third of the canvas like a stabilizing band. Though it is small in scale, we can make out clearly the details of ships proceeding into the harbor and at rest within. We are able to recognize key buildings within the city, monuments of church and state: the towers of the cathedral and the convent to the left, and to the right the shapes of Morro Castle guarding the harbor. As the foreground figures seem to cant in a V-shape toward the viewer, where the nose of the shark and the hand of Watson almost meet, so the recession of the harbor toward its entrance presents an opposing and balancing V-shape. But where the former is abrupt and confusing, the latter is clear, enclosing space logically; and against the recession in three dimensions stands the clear repetitive pattern of verticals and horizontals, the cathedral cross echoed in numerous crosstrees of the receding masts, as if promising certainty, a definable world, and even ultimate security to the perceiver. Thus our perception of the background taps a very different kind of eighteenth-century aesthetic experience: of the topographical tradition, the harborscape, marine view, localized and made identifiable, stable, and recognizable by reference to a "real" world of objects beyond the self of the perceiver. As the Sublime asks for ultimate definition within the mind, the topographical reassures us of the reality of the perceivable external world.[5]

What reconciles and, to a degree, harmonizes these conflicting aesthetic experiences is of course the great central

plane of the canvas: the boat and its occupants. Spatially it
stabilizes the canvas: the line of the oar and the boathook
harpoon which run beyond the edge of the canvas lock the
boat in place in two dimensions; the two figures reaching toward Watson extend us almost into the nightmare world of
the foreground, while the two standing figures almost fill up
the apex of the background-V and close off the harbor. Both
the enclosing shape of the boat and the traditional classical
pyramidal organization of the figures in the middle ground
give us the full experience of three-dimensional human space
denied in both fore- and background. They become the focus
of visual order and, we come to realize, of dramatic resolution;
for the boatsmen will be the saving of Watson and the destruction of the shark. The central boat scene imposes a principle of classical order upon foreground and background,
linking all three.

The point of such an analysis of our visual experience of
Watson and the Shark is ultimately not only what it yields on
a formal level but what it suggests. The dominant impression
which the *Watson* leaves is that of a willfully *achieved* effect,
a momentary reconciliation of dissonant impulses, gesturally
melodramatic and stylistically discordant rather than visually
harmonious. One has only to compare the *Watson* to those
works with which it has been frequently associated, like one
of the great baroque *Lion Hunts* of Rubens or Gericault's
Raft of the Medusa (1818–19) to see that both of those have
a unity and harmony of style which the *Watson* lacks. Or, to
put the issue more positively, the aesthetic significance of the
achieved "style" of the *Watson* lies precisely in its harnessing
together of contrary impulses, in its eclectic use of varying
aesthetic conventions of often contradictory meaning to try
to reconcile the sublimity of the sea with the order of land,
the harmonies of the humanly created with the chaos of unmediated nature, through an act of heroic will—a will enacted
by both the painter and his central subjects in the boat. In

both the tenuous balance created on the canvas and in the belief which this symbolically defines, that men in boats can create an order which is neither the dull rectilinearities of the shore nor those vast regions of the deep which suggest the possibility, as Melville was to tell us, that "the invisible spheres were formed in fright," Copley's *Watson* is visually a key statement of its own particular moment of 1778.[6]

It is my contention that our eclectic experience of the *Watson* is not accidental but a function of the various forces which converge to create this work and our experience of it; that in some sense the dissonances we perceive express the inadequacy of traditional conventions of style to give shape to Copley's sense of his subject and of his need to find—and, we may say, with hindsight, to help to create—a new style in American art. That Copley himself may have been self-consciously aware of only some of the forces which shaped his work is surely true. The concern with the intellectual and aesthetic context of the creative act is the task of the critic and historian, not the creator. Yet the visual evidence cries for some kind of explanation, and our task becomes thus the understanding of the aesthetic choices open to Copley and to the American artist more generally at this particular juncture in American history.

II. The Grand Style

The first and most direct clues are biographical and lie in the significance of the *Watson* commission in 1778 to Copley's career. At the age of forty Copley had a well-deserved reputation as a portrait painter. Twenty years of effort in colonial Boston had made him a master of the realistic depiction of surfaces and textures, of the personality and position of a wide range of American individuals, and it was quickly apparent to Copley both before he left London in 1774 on his continental tour and when he returned there in 1776 that he would not want for subjects upon whom to practice his craft and support his growing family. But Europe meant more to Copley than the production of likenesses for wealthy sitters. As early as 1765, as a young Bostonian he had submitted to an astonished Joshua Reynolds and Benjamin West in London his glowing *Boy with a Squirrel*. The message of Europe that had returned to him was the double one of praise for his great native accomplishment as a portraitist coupled with the lure of the great tradition: "nothing is wanting to Perfect you now but a Sight of what has been done by the great Masters, and if you Could make a viset to Europe for this Porpase. . . ." In 1774 he had finally succumbed, and the record of his travel and study in England and on the continent in the two years that followed is one of excited discovery of the great tradition of Western painting: of Titian and Rubens, of Michelangelo and Correggio, and perhaps above all, of Raphael.[7]

The visual experience of the great works and of the possibility of extending himself in theme and form beyond portraiture was powerfully reinforced by his contact with men like West and Sir Joshua in London, Gavin Hamilton and Piranesi in Rome. If his letters to his young step-brother the painter Henry Pelham are any indication, the most powerful shaping force of these years of travel and study were the *Discourses on Art* which Reynolds had been delivering to the newly-formed Royal Academy, for Copley repeatedly urged Pelham to secure them [8] and in his advice to Pelham echoed Reynolds again and again. Most important, perhaps, he found encouragement in Reynolds, who was himself a portraitist, to reach beyond his parochial limits towards the grand style.

The early *Discourses* thus provide us with important evidence of how neoclassical aesthetics, in their finest formulation, were of use to the colonial American artist. In the second *Discourse* Reynolds had spoken of the three stages of the artist's growth. Of the first—the period of learning the skills of the craft: drawing, color, design—Copley was surely already a master. Indeed craftsmanship was the strength of the colonial limner tradition, and its limitation. The second stage consisted of collecting subjects for expression. Reynolds distinctly did not mean by this a list of sitters for portraits but rather the amassing of "a stock of ideas, to be combined and varied as occasion may require" by studying the great works of the past to seek after perfection as it was partially embodied in a variety of examples, so that the general idea emerging might therefore "regulate his taste, and enlarge his imagination." [9] This was, of course, what had brought Copley to Europe after much urging and advice from Benjamin West, and what he was setting out to do in his European travels. Reynolds' advice thus was particularly *a propos*.[10]

The third stage, wherein the artist absorbed the lessons of past art and went on to create original works, in Reynolds' words, "emancipates the Student from subjection to any authority, but what he shall himself judge to be supported by reason" (p. 26). This was heady language indeed to a Bostonian in 1774! *Watson and the Shark* would be the great early evidence that Copley understood it in aesthetic terms; but what of its distinctly political overtones? At this moment, with politics at a distance (though constantly reminded of it by letters from home), Copley had enough to worry about professionally. The *Discourses* made it very clear that he must transcend his past. Portrait painting was a low and limited form of art (pp. 52, 70), and those qualities of minuteness, fidelity to fact, to the local, to the ornamental, to contemporary truth in which Copley had excelled, Reynolds repeatedly declared to be at best limiting, at worst vulgar and degrading to great art (pp. 58–60, 48–49). This extended even to accessories: "It is the inferior stile that marks the variety of stuffs." For the historical painter, "the cloathing is neither woollen, nor linen, nor silk, sattin, or velvet: it is drapery;

it is nothing more" (p. 62). These harsh words ran counter
to all that Boston had seemed to praise in the colonial portraitist's work.[11]

And yet Reynolds shared the Lockean basis of Copley's
American aesthetics. Again and again the *Discourses* made
clear the visual empiricism which underlay the ideal criteria.
For Reynolds the grand style was not the function of some
innate idea but was drawn from the rich and varied experience of the eye with the perceptible world of nature and
works of past art. Thus Copley in Rome argued to Pelham
after Reynolds and the Lockean manner the compatibility
of the real and the ideal, for the ideal was itself a form of
memory: stored past perception.[12]

What was eminently clear from reading the *Discourses* was
that the way for Copley to move beyond his limitations as a
portrait painter was through accomplishment in a higher
form of art: history painting. Copley was not four days arrived from America before West took him to see *The Death
of Wolfe*, his own major breakthrough in that vein,[13] and the
challenge was clear. But how was this reorientation to be accomplished? The path lay through the Vatican, and Reynolds
described the journey in the first *Discourse:*

> RAFFAELLE, it is true, had not the advantage of studying in an
> Academy; but all Rome, and the works of MICHAEL ANGELO in
> particular, were to him an Academy. On the sight of the
> CAPELLA SISTINA, he immediately from a dry, Gothick, and even
> insipid manner, which attends to the minute accidental discrimi-
> nations of particular and individual objects, assumed that grand
> style of painting, which improves partial representation by the
> general and invariable ideas of nature. (pp. 15–16).

Reynolds' advice to study Raphael was already a commonplace when he uttered it, but to Copley it must have seemed
a personal allegory, clear and immediate; for the limitations
which Reynolds ascribed to Raphael's early work were precisely those which Benjamin West had reported back to the

young Copley in 1765 ("to[o] liney") when the *Boy with a Squirrel* had been submitted to Reynolds and public exhibition in London.[14] Copley's career in the years 1774–1778 attest to the literalness with which he read the allegory. His letters are full of Reynoldsian praise of Raphael, of his study of the Vatican frescoes and the great Cartoons, and of Raphael's technique as draughtsman as well, all as it related to his own work. It was during his Roman stay that Copley painted *The Ascension* (Fig. 2), drawing on the lessons learned from study of what most eighteenth-century critics were agreed was Raphael's greatest work: *The Transfiguration* (Fig. 3). Two years after he returned to London he expressed again his debt to the divine Sanzio in *Watson and the Shark*.[15]

The opportunity was a fortunate one. In a letter from Parma of 22 June 1775 he had confided to Pelham that "portrait painting I shall pursue, unless tempted to some things in history by any that may wish to imploy me in that way." But though *The Ascension* and a *Nativity* record his explorations into traditional religious themes and a *Priam Beseeching Achilles* testifies to his responsiveness to the classical muse, as it had been expounded by West, Gavin Hamilton, and the Winckelmann group in Rome, it was the commission from Brook Watson which marks the major breakthrough and his contribution to what Edgar Wind has called "the revolution of history painting." [16]

Watson and the Shark looks both to the past and the future; it gathers up the Raphaelesque tradition of history painting as Copley had absorbed it both directly and through Reynolds, and then pushes it forward toward the revolution of which America was both the fact and symbol. In an important sense, the *Watson* was an "imitation," as Reynolds had articulated that concept in the sixth *Discourse* in part to counteract the increasingly attractive notion that art is a product of inspiration, of native genius alone. (The idea of the "American

Scholar" emerging out of "unhandselled savage nature" would attract later American artists, but clearly it did not attract Copley.) Reynoldsian imitation was not slavish copying but creative absorption of the nature and art of the past. As Reynolds said of Raphael: "It is from his having taken so many models, that he became himself a model for all succeeding painters; always imitating, and always original." [17]

The astonishing thing about the *Watson*, in this sense, is not its bold originality but its creative imitation, the degree to which Copley understood and absorbed the tradition and refashioned it to his own purposes. His letters to Pelham record the process: "I frequently studied the works of Raphaiel, etc., and by that kept the fire of the Imagination alive and made it my object to produce a work that might stand by any others." The context here is his key letter of 1775 which instructs Pelham in historical composition by retracing his own process in *The Ascension*. More important for our purposes, the letter indicates how well he had understood Reynolds' lessons: that his own originality was enhanced, not threatened, by the study of Raphael. Raphael could and did teach him the great lessons of figural placement in large compositions, of making forms expressive of some "General Idea," of subordinating the particular detail (on which, as a New England portraitist, he had lavished such beautiful attention) to the effect of the whole, and of how to imitate past art in order to achieve his own originality of statement.[18] The specific lessons of Raphael were carried back to London and incorporated into the *Watson*.

"Invention in Painting," said Reynolds, "does not imply the invention of the subject; for that is commonly supplied by the Poet or Historian" (p. 57). Yet in a literal sense, Copley's subject was supplied by the anecdote of his patron, Brook Watson. "With respect to the choice," Reynolds continued,

Fig. 2. John Singleton Copley. *The Ascension*. 1775. oil on canvas. 32 x 29 inches. Courtesy, Museum of Fine Arts, Boston. Bequest of Susan Greene Dexter in memory of Charles and Martha Babcock Amory.

"no subject can be proper that is not generally interesting. It ought to be either some eminent instance of heroick action, or heroick suffering. There must be something either in the action, or in the object, in which men are universally concerned, and which powerfully strikes upon the publick sympathy" (p. 57). Did the *Watson* qualify?

From the conservative point of view of the *Discourses* clearly it did not, for Reynolds had gone on to say that by universally interesting he meant Greek and Roman history and scriptural stories. The recent incident that Copley had been commissioned to depict was thus in Reynoldsian terms in danger of being "degraded by the vulgarisms of ordinary life in any country" (p. 58). Yet the new voices of the 1770s were arguing to the contrary: that by removing one's subject to a distant place, if not a distant time, it might be brought within the acceptable canons. But Copley was not, like West in the *Death of Wolfe* or *Penn's Treaty with the Indians*, dealing with an "eminent" heroic figure. Brook Watson was merely a wealthy merchant and the incident smacked of lurid reportage.[19] If herein lay part of Copley's boldness, his "imitation" lay in drawing from the local its general idea: the conflict between man and the overwhelming power of nature.

The great tradition surely offered examples of this larger theme: the *Laocoön* was only the best known among classical examples;[20] *St. George and the Dragon* perhaps the most obvious Christian type.[21] Raphael could offer Copley more direct assistance. With an instinct for the dynamic nature of his own material, Copley turned not to the great earlier more static compositions of Raphael like the *Disputa* or the *School of Athens* but to Raphael's later work in the Stanza d'Eliodoro, the Cartoons, the Loggias, and to that work which Heinrich Wölfflin has called "his last word on the grand style in narrative painting," *The Transfiguration. The Expulsion of Helio-*

Fig. 3. Raphael Sanzio. *The Transfiguration.* 1518–23. oil on panel. 159 x 109 inches. Vatican Museum, Rome. Photo Alinari.

dorus offered one model of the sprawling human figure just
before he is trampled by the animal—in this case the white
horse of the avenging angel. In the Cartoon of *The Death of
Ananias* another helpless figure sprawls in the foreground before overwhelming power—here, the power of the Word.
The tapestry of *The Conversion of St. Paul* in the Vatican
offered but one more example. Both in basic idea and in figural
placement, Raphael's late work offered to Copley a number
of general sources to "imitate." [22]

Rubens' *Lion Hunt*, a print after which Copley owned at
some point in his career, may also have been, as others have
pointed out, a source upon which Copley drew in the creation
of the *Watson*, for Reynoldsian imitation urged the artist not
to copy any one master but to draw inspiration from all. But
Copley in the *Watson* is surely far from being a "Rubeniste"
in any larger sense. Although the central motif of this canvas
was more dynamic than one usually finds in either Nicholas
Poussin or West, Copley organized the *Watson* in three
distinct planes or bands rather than with the fully three-
dimensional spatial articulation of the Rubeniste baroque. He
combined as late Raphael did the dynamics of a central story
action with a stable—in Copley almost a frozen—middle and
background.[23] And quite obviously, in his limited range of
color in the *Watson* Copley had heeded Reynolds' advice to
beware of the excessive brilliance of Venetian (and, by extension, Rubeniste) coloring, and to strive instead for "that
solidity, steadiness, and simplicity of effect, which heroick
subjects require, and which simple or grave colours only can
give to a work" (p. 66).

It has also been suggested recently and less convincingly
that the figure of Watson himself is a mirror image of the
statue of the gladiator in the Villa Borghese.[24] If so, Copley
was surely punning on his source, since the figure of Watson
is one of helplessness before the power of nature, not com-
bativeness. What seems more likely as a specific source and

inspiration for the figure—in the twist of its torso and the position of the legs, arms, and even fingers, and especially in the "General Idea" of the figure's helplessness; indeed, in all save its apparent age—is the figure of the deranged child in the lower section of Raphael's *Transfiguration* (Fig. 3). This was a truly creative use of imitation, for the dramatic situation of the miracle of the child restored (as in Copley's *Watson*, the moment we see is just before the child's "rescue") is a notable instance, as gladiatorial combat distinctly is not, of what the generation of Copley called "The Sublime." Though generally Raphael was identified in the late eighteenth century as the apostle of the Beautiful and Michelangelo of the Sublime, the *Transfiguration* was clearly an exception to the rule,[25] and Copley's borrowing in this case but gives further evidence of his attempt to identify the foreground of his canvas with sublime seeing. We will return to the significance of the iconological differences between Copley's secular painting and its sources in the religious art of Raphael. At this point what is important are the ways in which the limited provincial American portraitist learned through Reynoldsian imitation to work in the grand style of history painting.

To say this is not in any way to minimize the boldness of Copley's achievement or the differences between *Watson and the Shark* and the conservative neoclassical theory that Reynolds was defending in the Royal Academy; for Copley's subject matter is arresting. He had translated a personal anecdote in the life of a private individual into a grand drama of the conflict between man and the sea. *Watson* is history painting of a very special kind. Unlike the great tradition of painting as he had experienced it in his travel on the continent, unlike the works of Hamilton or David or Benjamin West or the ideal theory of Reynolds or Winckelmann, Copley's painting neither goes back to some great historic moment in secular or religious time nor focuses, as West did in the *Death of Wolfe* (1771) or *Penn's Treaty* (1772) or as David would with

Napoleon, upon great heroes of the recent past. Copley's sense seemed to tell him that the grand style was appropriate to the ordinary man, that it needed neither the clothing of the antique nor the associated grandeur of a great name or historic event. In this respect alone, Copley was challenging any neat hierarchical theory of genres and consciously mixing the modes. A common sea anecdote becomes through Copley's treatment, rather than through its allusive or associative appeal only, a drama in the grand style. The value of the local and the real, the validity of the particular, is asserted and reconciled with the ideal. There is surely in this very assertion—however implicit—of the larger value of the local, the germ of a new aesthetic, one with great implications for later American art.

For the present, in his insistence on recentness of time if not of space, in his localized harbor background, in the lack of eminence in the central figures, and in his sea subject, Copley was contributing notably to the revolution of history painting which was taking place in the 1770s, spearheaded by Americans like West and Copley, whose aesthetic premises were more open, flexible, and experimental, as their political premises and experience were not based upon rigid notions of rank or slavish adherence to precedent. British acceptance of the crucial role of the Americans is worth noting. In 1783, just as the Revolutionary War was ending, the Corporation of London sought advice about a painting to memorialize the British defeat of the Spanish at Gibraltar. They consulted only two painters: West and Copley.[26]

The fixed hierarchy of genres was breaking down in the 1770s and with it the class bias that was its political basis. Copley was careful in the *Watson* not to individualize the faces too much—to concentrate on general expressiveness and to avoid portraiture. But the *Watson* clearly does not accept Sir Joshua's aristocratic premise that "each person should also have that expression which men of his rank generally exhibit"

(p. 61). For Copley the American this view was untenable; in his pictorial organization of the canvas, the harpooner and the Negro share the honors at the top of the pyramid. Copley's European study had led him to follow Reynoldsian principles to American ends. It had emancipated him "from subjection to any authority, but what he shall himself judge to be supported by reason."

III. Seascape

If one turns from stylistic problems more directly to thematic ones, Copley's relation to his American world comes more clearly into focus, for *Watson and the Shark* is a seascape. Whether Copley's attempt in the *Watson* to create a seascape as his first major venture into the grand style occurred only through the happy coincidence of Brook Watson's appearance with the commission for this particular scene or whether Copley was attracted to the challenge of depicting the great conflict of man with the sea we will probably never know. Copley's personal feelings about the sea remain somewhat obscure. As a boy whose childhood was spent in his father's house on the Long Wharf in the bustling port town of Boston, Copley's exposure to the maritime world was early and direct, but there seems to be no concrete evidence of his attitudes. His early painting suggests, for its part, an attempt to distance himself from the direct experiencing of the sea and to substitute various available conventions that would aesthetically frame the maritime world. Thus a childhood anecdote speaks of his drawing the children of Israel crossing the Red Sea painted in "the deepest and most brilliant shades of red." Interestingly, two of the earliest paintings that have come down to us, which Copley did around 1754 as apprenticeship exercises from existing prints, are based on traditional classical iconography of the sea: *The Return of Neptune* and *Galatea Triomphe Sur l'Onde*. Although many of

Copley's American portraits were of men involved in one way or another with the maritime world, only rarely did Copley connect these men visually with the sea. In the few cases, like the *Thomas Greene* (1758), *Nicholas Boylston* (1767), or *John Amory* (1768) portraits, where he did do so, he used the available pattern of a sea-boat-harbor scene glimpsed through a window or behind a curtain with which the sitter does not in any way dynamically interact, for the pictorial convention was clearly designed to subordinate and limit the image of the sea, to control and frame it in human terms.[27]

How and when Copley heard of the incident in Brook Watson's youth which formed the subject of his first major seascape painting is again not clear.[28] What is clear is that when the commission came, he used it as a challenge not only to reshape the tradition of history painting but also to break free of his own limited use of traditional seascape conventions and thus contributed in a crucial way to the development of American seascape art. For despite Copley's own limited exploration of its possibilities before the *Watson*, seascape as an aesthetic mode of apprehending and bringing under control the sea as subject matter had already by 1778 a considerable background in America upon which Copley or any artist, in words or in paint, could draw. In the nineteenth century—in the hands of writers like Cooper, Poe, Dana, Melville, and Whitman, or of painters like Allston, Birch, Lane, Heade, Homer, and Ryder—seascape was to become a dominant American aesthetic mode. The *Watson* stands at a crucial turning point between the limited achievement of colonial artists in the mode in the years before the Revolution and the great achievements of our artists and writers in the age to come.

The passage across the Atlantic had been, of course, the great fact of the colonizing experience, uprooting men and women from the known world and carrying them to the unknown. The voyage itself was filled with unknown terrors, especially in the earliest years. But the seventeenth-century literary artist,[29] especially in Copley's New England, had used the fact of the sea experience in a variety of fruitful ways to explore the aesthetic possibilities of an American seascape and to turn it to human and spiritual use. Drawing upon a fund of classical, medieval, and Renaissance notions of the sea, the epic quest, and the search for Terra Incognita, the American Puritans reshaped these to their own spiritual needs and produced a substantial body of what may be called typological seascapes in a variety of forms—history, travel, personal literature, poetry—through which the actual was reshaped in imaginative terms. In the process, the Atlantic Ocean became, for example, the Red Sea, or the flimsy bark the ship of the faithful in the hands of the Ultimate Pilot who would reveal to the voyagers "the Wonders of the Deep" on their way to a typologically conceived promised land. Puritan theology offered the first century of New Englanders a way of finding a rich imaginative language for understanding and giving shape to their experience with the sea, because it offered a well-articulated system of ontological and eschatological certainty against which the uncertainties and indeed the terrors of the experienced could be measured. From Bradford's *Plimouth Plantation* to Cotton Mather's *Magnalia Christi Americana* of 1702, the providential vision gave the Puritans a way of coming to terms with their dislocating experience of the sea, of turning uncertainty into spiritual knowledge, doubt into hosannas of praise to the glory of God.[30]

Mather's *Magnalia* is a kind of epic summation of the tradition at the beginning of the eighteenth century, as well as a previsioning of things to come. The sixth book, of "Remarkables of the Divine Providence Among the People of New-England," sets as its task the recording of "all extraordinary things wherein the existence and agency of the *invisible world* is more sensibly demonstrated." That this was more than just another pious accumulation of miracles becomes quickly evident in Mather's prefatory remarks, for in taking up the task begun by others, including his father Increase in the *Illustrious Providences* (1684), Cotton directs his compendium especially to those critics, deists, and doubters who question whether it is Divine Providence or chance, "incerto curso," $\tau\nu\chi\eta$, "blind *fortune*," that directs human destiny. At just the point where the Lockean epistemological revolution is insisting upon the experiential basis of all knowledge, Mather undertakes to demonstrate in "sensible" terms the "evident"—that is, sensibly apparent—"operations of the Almighty God, 'whose kingdom ruleth over all.'" [31]

Naturally he begins, as had his father before him, with a chapter "Relating Wonderful Sea-Deliverances" entitled "Christus Super Aquas," for as he notes, "they 'that go down to the sea in ships, these do see the works of the Lord and his wonders in the deep'" (p. 343, citing Ps. 107.23–24). The chapter's motto is from that point in the third book of the *Aeneid* where Aeneas sets sail from Crete, convinced now that the prophecies demand that the exiles re-establish their great cities and empires of the future in the place the Greeks call Hesperia, the land to the West.[32] The implications were clear to Mather's readers: classical Roman epic paralleled and reinforced the Old Testament quest of the chosen people for the promised land, and both confirm and prevision the spatial journey of the Puritans "super aquas" to America and the ultimate spiritual journey of the Christian soul to the City of God. Here specifically in terms of seascape, as throughout the *Magnalia* in more general terms, Mather played a crucial role in accommodating and reconciling richly and fully the intellectual and aesthetic heritage of Christian and classical antiquity. The importance of this strategy in an age that would come to be called "neoclassic," demanding of its audiences that they understand themselves in Greek and Roman terms, can hardly be overestimated. At this particular point in the *Magnalia*, for example, those who knew their *Aeneid* could hold in their minds the remembered image of the stormy seas which Aeneas encounters in the lines immediately following the motto when Mather undertakes to "carry my reader upon the huge Atlantick" (p. 243).

His first story, "A Pious Anchorite," tells of one Ephriam Howe who sails from New Haven to Boston, is driven to sea by wild storms, loses both his sons to the tempest (and without the comfort granted to the biblical Ephriam of friends on shore [1 Chron. 7:22]). In trying to decide whether to strive "for the New England shore, or bear away for the southern islands" (p. 344; the North-South alternatives are worth noting), "they first sought unto God by earnest prayer in this difficult case, and then determined the difficulty by casting a lot" (p. 344). Mather seems intent upon emphasizing his doubter's problem here, by giving thus the initial victory to chance, but subsequent events more than redress the balance. Howe is cast on the rocks off Cape Sable but (like Christ on the Sea of Galilee) "*God made that storm a calm; so that the waves were still*" (p. 344; Ps. 107.29, Matt. 8.26), and they make their way to shore. In time the others die and Howe is left alone on his deserted island. First bewailing his sins and his fate, he turns at last to giving "*thanks* unto God for the marvelous preservations which he had hitherto experienced" (p. 345) and is *immediately* thereafter saved by a ship and returned to his family in New Haven. In a few brief pages Mather has economically but vividly rendered his story, balanced well-selected detail of man's human experience against the ultimate pattern. Realism and typology are artfully interwoven into an aesthetic whole.

The other stories, of terrors natural and human, of shipwrecks and pirates, of Northern tempests and West Indian islands with crocodiles and savages, mitigated not by divine intervention but by divine guidance, confirm the pattern. Mather's narrative seascapes suggest the richness and vitality of the mode which would open up to full fictional form in the eighteenth century in works that range from *Robinson Crusoe* (1719) to William Williams' *Penrose* (1770s?) and Royall Tyler's *Algerine Captive* (1797) at the end of the century.

Copley's *Watson* illuminates what has occurred to transform the pattern in the intervening years. In the context of European history painting, the action of the *Watson* has been characterized as a traditional "mirabilia," a visible wonder; and undoubtedly in that context and to its English audience its appeal may have been in the reportorial excitement of the shark scene in the far-off exotic place called the West Indies.[33] But to the providential mentality of New England, to understand this scene thus as a quaint oddity was to submit to blind Fortune rather than to understand the workings of Jehovah. One may suggest that in its American context *Watson and the Shark* is a remarkable deliverance and contributes implicitly to the debate about the relation of nature to the divine.

The youth in the picture has already been passed twice by the shark; in the second pass the shark has ripped off his right foot above the ankle. Just as he is coming in for the kill, Watson will be saved by the men in the boat. The implicit conceit, in secular terms, is "saved to go on to lead a prosperous life as a prominent London merchant." What is missing is any clear sense of theological context: that it is God's providence that will save young Watson. Copley's Raphael-esque visual sources all pointed to that religious resolution: Heliodorus is driven from the temple by the angelic horseman, Ananias struck dead by the word of God. The two figures bending out of the boat to grasp the net in the Cartoon for *The Miraculous Draught of Fishes* may have been a suggestive source for the two figures leaning forward towards Watson, but the meaning has been reversed: the fish is not here gathered as symbol and miracle of the Christ but is the terror from the deep. Finally, the deranged child in the *Transfiguration* (Fig. 3) will be saved by the vision of the floating

Christ who dominates the upper half of the picture, but *Watson and the Shark* both in visual and intellectual terms lacks the upper range of the *Transfiguration*. In his earlier *Ascension* (Fig. 2) Copley had tried to present the two realms of experience, the human and the divine, but the result had been awkward.[34] The space between the strong horizontal band of the gathered apostles and angels and the floating Christ is too great. The Raphaelesque gestures of the figures and certain rising lines in the landscape and clouds do not pull the whole together into a unified vision, as Raphael had in the *Transfiguration*. The visual difference suggests a difference in the way Raphael and Copley conceive of man's relation to the Divine. In pictorial terms Raphael suggests a complex interrelationship, Copley that God is above and beyond man, and identified, as Americans in the century following were increasingly to identify him, with space.[35]

In Copley's more successful effort in the grand style, *Watson and the Shark*, the miracle is effected not by a transfigured Christ but by men in a boat. The dimensions of the canvas and the three strong bands of action—Watson-shark, the boat, the harbor scene—give the work pictorially a strongly horizontal orientation, and Copley emphasizes this fact by brutally chopping off the powerful vertical line of the boathook. The importance of Copley's aesthetic choice in 1778 is made particularly clear by comparing the original version with his later vertical version of 1782 (Fig. 4). The details of the two are almost identical but the change in proportions has radically altered the vision. The whole effect of the 1782 replica is of a distanced experience: the shark and Watson are not immediately threatening to the viewer and the eye can travel upward as the boathook vertical carries us to the sky above. The organization is more traditional—in a European sense—and it is clearly both less arresting and less American, as John Mc-Coubrey has rightly argued.[36] What is compelling about the original is precisely its immediacy, its "forced" quality, its in-

sistence that the conflict of man with the sea must be played out horizontally, in the interplay of the sublime foreground, the human middle ground, and the topographical background.[37] Copley has, in effect, reversed the traditional pattern. If there is a power of the divine in Copley's *Watson and the Shark* it comes not from any transcendent realm above the human but from the depths of the sea.

By identifying the foreground action of his painting with the Sublime, Copley was identifying it with that aesthetic experience of God working not through the order and beauty of his harmonious universe but made visible in his unadulterated might and power, his unmediated glory. As Burke had helped to redefine the concept, the Sublime existed as a quality of objects that could not be separated fully from our perception of them. What this means for us in terms of Copley's *Watson* is that the forceful jamming of the foreground close to the picture plane involves us as viewers, as it involves those close to us in the boat, in sublime perceiving, not merely in the recognition of a sublime object (or a "mirabilia"). Copley's canvas thus suggests that man faces the Sublime as it emerges with the face of terror from the sea, from Nature herself, not from any ineffable transfigured Christ; that if it strikes terror to the soul of Watson (and of the viewer), man's appropriate response to it is not worship or prayer but an act of human will—Ahab's "Thy right worship is defiance." [38] The *Watson* transfers the "saving" function from God's will to that of the human community, both individually and collectively, both as a group of men striving in the rescuing boat and as the ship and harbor world from which they come and which serves as a kind of architectural surround that closes off space and offers precisely the order, clarity, and serenity which the foreground so vehemently denies.

Fig. 4. John Singleton Copley. *Watson and the Shark*. 1782. oil on canvas. 36 x 30½ inches. The Detroit Institute of Arts. Purchase; the Dexter M. Ferry, Jr. Fund.

Copley thus effected pictorially in the *Watson* a radical reorientation of the iconography which he borrowed from the
grand tradition of Raphael. Furthermore, by emphasizing sublime perception rather than the recognition of innately sublime objects or figures, like the transfigured Christ or the
shark *per se*, Copley's *Watson* suggests a wholly different attitude toward aesthetic experience from either Cotton Mather's
historical recording of remarkable providences or Benjamin
West's historical tableaux, to be understood statically, in their
innate ulterior significance, after the fact. What seems like a
shift in emphasis in Copley's aesthetic premises could become,
in the hands of a Joseph Mallord Turner or an Edgar Allan
Poe, a radically transformed aesthetic where the object quite
literally dissolves before the sublime perceptions of the creator
and observer. Copley would probably have been appalled by
this possibility. He was not even willing to go as far as Benjamin West would in *Death on a Pale Horse* and related explorations of the Sublime in the coming years.[39] To be "emancipated from subjection to any authority, but what he shall
judge to be supported by reason" did not mean to Copley giving oneself solipsistically to the Sublime. There is a crucial
difference between the romantic achievements of Coleridge
and Turner, Poe and Ryder, and Copley's recasting of the
traditional iconography, much as it liberated him from subjection to the authority of his sources. The precarious but
reasoned willful balance which Copley achieved in the *Watson* marks it as a paradigmatic achievement of the 1770s rather
than as a rime of the New World mariner.

IV. An American Identity

The secularization of aesthetic meaning and of seascape in
particular, of which *Watson and the Shark* is such a stunning
graphic instance, had been taking place throughout the eighteenth century in a variety of forms. The Puritan meditative

verse of Edward Taylor, based upon the typologizing of
Noah and Jonah, became the bland neoclassical "Hymn at
Sea" (1732) of Mather Byles, immediately turned into parody
by Joseph Green in his "Lines on Byles's Voyage" (1733).
Ebeneezer Cook romped briskly through the clichés of the
voyage ("Shock'd by the Terrors of the Main . . .") to a
satirizing of the whole colonial venture in "The Sot-Weed
Factor" (1708). Prose travel literature increasingly focused
on the data of natural history rather than its supernatural
ends or on adventures for their own sake. And both of these
in turn affected the tradition of remarkable deliverances. The
novel emerged in the eighteenth century in part out of the
transformation of Bunyan's Puritan allegorical journey into
the fictional form of Defoe's *Robinson Crusoe*. It seems likely
that William Williams, best known today as Benjamin West's
first teacher and as a portrait painter in colonial Philadelphia
and New York, had with him at least a draft of his contribution to the new genre, *Journal of Penrose, Seaman*, when he
returned to England on the eve of the Revolution. If so, this
"first American novel" bears all the hallmarks, albeit in rather
loose and rough form, of the new shape of American seascape:
the pseudo-autobiographical form, which drew upon Williams' own adventures as a shipwrecked sailor in Central
America, upon travel literature, upon some residue of the
Bunyan-Defoe tradition coupled with sporadic usage of the
conventions of the sublime sea. What is most notable for our
purposes, perhaps, is Williams' depiction of the idyllic, almost
pastoral community that Penrose creates with the Nicaraguan
Indians, which serves as an emotional and intellectual center
of harmony against which to measure the violence, both natural and human, of the European maritime world.[40]

Because the art of New England in the seventeenth century
had been so strongly religious in character, the secularizing of
the forms of seascape had a special importance in the colonies,
though the new forms themselves were not notably different,

where they were not directly borrowed, from those of the mother country. Furthermore, the emphasis in Copley's *Watson and the Shark* on the saving function of the sea-going community in the boat also had a special resonance in the America of 1778. However unintentionally, the forms of the *Watson* clarify the new sense of American identity as it emerged in the 1770s.

Characteristically, the formulation of that identity came from European observers. While Copley was laboring in Rome to master the grand style of history painting, Edmund Burke was addressing the House of Commons in the grand style of oratory, attempting to bring his colleagues to a sense of the present historic meaning of the American experience. In his plea for conciliation of 22 March 1775, he searched for an image to crystallize the significance of the New World and found it in the American confrontation with the sea.

He began by appealing to British self-interest but quickly passed beyond the economic value of the fisheries into the rhetoric of the Sublime: "And pray, Sir, what in the world is equal to it?" (Melville would pick up this phrase as one of the "Extracts" for *Moby-Dick*.) "Pass by the other parts, and look at the manner in which the people of New England have of late carried on the whale-fishery.

> Whilst we follow them among the tumbling mountains of ice, and behold them penetrating into the deepest frozen recesses of Hudson's Bay and Davis's Straits, whilst we are looking for them beneath the arctic circle, we hear that they have pierced into the opposite region of polar cold, that they are at the antipodes, and engaged under the frozen serpent of the South. Falkland Island, which seemed too remote and romantic an object for the grasp of national ambition, is but a stage and resting-place in the progress of their victorious industry.[41]

The seagoing race Burke describes seems ubiquitous: "No sea but what is vexed by their fisheries. No climate that is not witness to their toils." And though a young race, a "recent

people . . . not yet hardened into the bone of manhood,"
Burke foresees for them a great destiny:

> When I contemplate these things—when I know that the
> colonies in general owe little or nothing to any care of ours,
> and that they are not squeezed into this happy form by the
> constraints of watchful and suspicious government, but that,
> through a wise and salutary neglect, a generous nature has been
> suffered to take her own way to perfection—when I reflect
> upon these effects, when I see how profitable they have been to
> us, I feel all the pride of power sink, and all presumption in the
> wisdom of human contrivances melt and die away within me—
> my rigor relents—I pardon something to the spirit of liberty.[42]

The passage must be quoted at such length because its impact
lies as much in the rhetorical form as in the content: in the
initial classical balance of his sentences which develop a cumu-
lative, finally an overwhelming "natural" power, before they
fall back finally and quietly upon the political word "liberty."
Burke presented his audience with a version of American vast-
ness, defined through American venturing on the sea. It is a
global destiny and the possibilities are not only economic but
visionary. Following "a generous nature" at its most perilous,
on the sea, is the way to "perfection"—the force of his rhetoric drives Burke to the ultimate formulation. Nature holds
the clue not only to American meaning but also to the "happy
form."

It would take a Melville or a Whitman to realize fully the
radical possibilities of the sea as an American political and
aesthetic form (and politics and aesthetics are inseparable for
both of those writers), but Burke was not alone in the 1770s
in his vision. During the same decade Hector St. John de
Crevecoeur was writing the essays that would be published in
1782 as *Letters from an American Farmer*. The *Letters* are
best known for their attempt to formulate the American
identity in the essay entitled "What is an American," and
Crevecoeur's ideal American is most often identified with

the sturdy yeoman. Though it is frequently overlooked, the "farmer" devotes fully a third of his book to the seagoing communities of Nantucket and Martha's Vineyard, hardly a yeoman's paradise.[43] Yet in terms of the final mythic structure of the *Letters*, these chapters play a crucial role. They are placed after Crevecoeur's early paeans to the pastoral ideal of the American farmer in the third letter, those "Western pilgrims" who "will finish the great circle" (p. 64) of culture which began in the East. He finds another image of the American, "this new man" (p. 63), in the figure of the discontented sailor who strips naked and swims ashore to find refuge in the new world (p. 83), and then goes on to the sketch of Andrew the Hebridean who leaves his barren island to find possibility in America. As Crevecoeur phrases it, "landing on this great continent is like going to sea" (p. 85).

But what is simile here becomes the literal truth in the five succeeding letters on the island fishermen. Crevecoeur focuses on the life of the inhabitants of Nantucket and the Vineyard not because they typify American life in any literal occupational sense but because, like Burke, he finds their experience archetypal. They embody his notion of the American as a risk-taking adventurer. Life for the American is not a being but a becoming, a process; a willing and choosing, not a result. The ocean experience is levelling; all participate in this common venture and all are functionally defined by it.

Yet it is more than this, for Crevecoeur's peroration to this section of the *Letters* in the eighth chapter moves beyond functional definitions of the American in occupational terms to a sublime meditation on the sea: "I had never before seen a spot better calculated to cherish contemplative ideas, perfectly unconnected with the great world, and far removed from its perturbations" (p. 157). The isolation of the coast of Nantucket comes to stand for the separation of America from the Old World and as such to generate ideas through the power of the sublime images of the sea:

The ever-raging ocean was all that presented itself to the view
. . . it irresistably attracted my whole attention: my eyes were
involuntarily directed to the horizontal line of that watery surface, which is ever in motion and ever threatening destruction
to these shores. My ears were stunned with the roar of its
waves. . . . My nostrils involuntarily inhaled the saline va-
pours. . . . My mind suggested a thousand vague reflections,
pleasing in the hour of their spontaneous birth, but now half
forgotten, and all indistinct; and who is the landman that can
behold without affright so singular an element, which by its im-
petuosity seems to be the destroyer of this poor planet, yet at
particular times accumulates the scattered fragments and pro-
duces islands and continents fit for men to dwell on! Who can
observe the regular vicissitudes of its waters without astonish-
ment. . . . (p. 157)

Beyond its ability to challenge human skill (Crevecoeur's description of a whale chase is particularly vivid [pp. 128–32])
or to meet human needs, the sea offers to sensory perception
images which can express his sense of amplitude, of horizontally limitless sublime possibility. In the confrontation with
the sea Crevecoeur finds at once an experience and an adequate
symbol of American national identity. The American sea is
both a means for shaping the New World community and a
sublime meaning in itself, something finally commensurate
to our capacity for wonder. That "spirit of liberty" which
Burke had rhetorically "pardoned something to" in his conciliation speech takes again the verbal and visual shape of
American seascape.

One returns thus to Copley's *Watson and the Shark* with a
heightened sense that, however limited the occasion of the
painting in Brook Watson's commission and however limited
Copley's conscious awareness and intent may have been in
this direction (and this we will never know), in his visual
accomplishment, in his organization of images on the canvas,
Copley captured a shared vision of the 1770s that American

identity was somehow inevitably linked to the sublime sea, and that what bound Americans together was their joint participation in risk-taking ventures against the minions of the deep. If the sublime terrors of the sea are dramatically placed for *our* sense perception in the foreground of Copley's canvas, the great central motif of the boat and its occupants offers us pictorially a powerful image of the New World community. The figures are interlocked both visually and functionally, some active, some poised for action, some contemplating the sublime scene before them. The boat is a strongly sculptured enclosure which supports and contains, even as it allows the extension of figures, oars, harpoon, and line beyond its confines. And it is strategically poised, an emissary from the orderly world of the shore into the sublime sea, willfully creating order in the middle ground.[44]

This middle position also finds its parallel in Crevecoeur's *Letters*, not only in the yeoman farmer's middle position between wild nature and the luxuries of coastal cities but also in the position of the vigorous Nantucket whalemen who venture into the sublime sea yet avoid, in their spartan society on shore, the corruptions of the city seaport. Crevecoeur's order of the middle ground is equally *willfully* created. The painter necessarily expresses this through spatial arrangement; Crevecoeur uses this pictorial technique for larger intellectual purposes, for to him the order symbolized by the farmer and the Nantucket is a constructed ideal order, a place of harmony where the New World realizes its promise. But it is surrounded by conflict. Recent scholarship on Crevecoeur has rightly emphasized the extent to which in the *Letters* Crevecoeur's theory of the middle way is constantly betrayed by his experience of dissonance, disharmony, and conflict.[45] In the light of this, the precarious balance of the middle ground emerges as Crevecoeur's statement of a mythic ideal, not of any comprehensive reality of the American world. That point is made implicitly in the movement from the seascape chapters abruptly to the chapter on "Charles Town" (Charleston, S.C.), with its rank odor of luxury, of profligacy, ending in the hideous image of the caged slave. The alternative to the sublime experience of free men choosing to adventure on the sea is the brutal entrapment of the Negro by his master. Freedom and slavery, extension into infinite space and enclosure: the pattern of the book is clear.

This suggests two final necessary questions regarding Copley's *Watson:* the significance of Havana and of the Negro in the boat. In some of our earlier considerations we have been associating the scene in Copley's picture with American identity, without differentiating Havana from the British colonies which were fighting for independence. Surely this is justifiable, for in all but the narrowly political sense forced by the alignments of the war and the Declaration of Independence, the West Indies were to the European imagination and, to a great extent, to the inhabitants of the thirteen mainland British colonies also, as much "America" as Massachusetts or South Carolina. Clearly, given Columbus, the West Indies had the priority of claim to the title and insofar as "America" meant some far-off exotic place, the exotic was more frequently associated with the tropical (or, occasionally, with the polar regions, to recall Burke's vision) than with the temperate climates of the English colonies: it was the "Bermoothes" of Shakespeare's *Tempest,* the desert isle of *Robinson Crusoe,* or *Penrose*'s Nicaraguan coast—in short, a tropical paradise. Even so ardent a political nationalist as Philip Freneau was inclined to find his ideal world not in New Jersey but in "The Beauties of Santa Cruz" (first published in 1779). The idea persisted because it represented a continuing quest for paradise in the western imagination. For John Locke in the seventeenth century, "In the beginning all the World was America." [46] In the eighteenth century the flood of information about America and the development of a bustling commercial society of risk-taking adventurers in

the British colonies could not help but undercut the image of
the exotic distant paradise. But the search persisted, sending
Melville's Tom to Taipee-Vai and Poe's Arthur Gordon Pym
to a south seas never-never land.

But if the southern alternative represented imaginatively a
kind of ideal counterculture to Northern commercialism, it
also meant Negro slavery. Havana was a key port in the
British slave trade, as any boy brought up on the Long Wharf
in Boston knew. Copley's imaginative feeling for this issue is
one of the unresolved problems of *Watson and the Shark*.[47]
It is a fact that Negroes normally formed a part of any ship's
complement of sailors. And it is also true, within its limits,
to say that the Negro in the rescuing boat is pictorially a conventional symbol of the exotic, to be found in Rubens' *Lion
Hunt* and related works.[48] But it is simply not enough to let
the issue rest thus in 1778, for pictorially the Negro plays a
crucial role in the painting. Moved back somewhat in space
from his original parallel position in an earlier sketch, his
head remains on a level with that of the white harpooner.
Against the violent thrusting action of the latter is balanced
his troubled contemplation of the scene. His left hand holds
the line, and his right hand, extended perhaps from having just
thrown the line, seems almost in a position of benediction.
Most important, perhaps, he alone is in direct touch with
Watson, through the sinewy curves of the line which runs
from his hand over the arm of Watson and separates in linear
terms Watson from the shark.[49]

We are in the presence of an occult symbolism the specific
meaning of which to Copley we have not penetrated. But its
suggestive power remains for us in the pictorial statement.
Not only is Copley's black man the democratic equal of the
whites; a symbolic relation exists between the strength and
heroic calm of the black and the eerie hue of white Watson,
tormented and helpless yet linked by the umbilicus—the
"monkey rope," in Melville's rephrasing of it—to his black

brother. The relationship which at its brutal worst is the caged Negro in Crevecoeur's Charles Town is transformed in the literature of the sea from Crusoe and Friday, master and slave, into Penrose, his native wife Luta and her brother Harry, into Fenimore Cooper's Dick Fid and S'ip or Miles Wallingford and Neb, and their apotheosis in the Ishmael-Queequeg relationship in *Moby-Dick*. Crevecoeur's assertion, that adventuring on the sea joins all Americans as equals, given symbolic statement in Copley's *Watson and the Shark*, is finally realized in full fictional form in the seascape literature of romantic America. That John Singleton Copley, comfortably ensconced in Leicester Square, London, in 1778, was consciously aware of the full symbolic import of his canvas seems unlikely, but it is one of the hallmarks of great works of art, like *Watson and the Shark* or *Moby-Dick*, that having been forged out of the materials of their time and place by an artist of great imaginative power, they do in fact reflect their age—transfigured.

ROGER B. STEIN

STATE UNIVERSITY OF NEW YORK

AT BINGHAMTON

Notes

1. Martha Babcock Amory, *The Domestic and Artistic Life of John Singleton Copley, R.A. . . .* (Boston: Houghton, Mifflin, 1882), p. 57; cf. ibid., p. 62.

2. Belknap to Rev. John Eliot, 1 May 1781, in *Massachusetts Historical Society Collections*, 6th Ser., 4 (Boston, 1891): 633b; cf. *Autobiography of Benjamin Franklin* (New Haven, Conn.: Yale Univ. Press, 1964), p. 257.

3. See Roger B. Stein, *John Ruskin and Aesthetic Thought in America, 1840–1900* (Cambridge, Mass.: Harvard Univ. Press, 1967), p. 9.

4. "Exhibition of the Royal Academy," *General Advertiser and Morning Intelligencer* [London], 27 April 1778, p. 4; for its source, see Edmund Burke, *Philosophical Enquiry into the Origin of our Ideas of the Sublime and Beautiful* [1st ed. 1757], ed. J. T. Boulton (London: Routledge & Kegan Paul; New York: Columbia Univ. Press, 1958), pp. 58–64 and *passim;* see

also the classic study by Samuel Holt Monk, *The Sublime: A Study of Critical Theories in XVIII-Century England* (1935; rpt. Ann Arbor: University of Michigan Press, Ann Arbor Paperbacks, 1960), and, especially, Ernest Lee Tuveson, *The Imagination as a Means of Grace: Locke and the Aesthetics of Romanticism* (Berkeley: Univ. of California Press, 1960), pp. 166–74.

5. On the topographical tradition, see Giuliano Briganti, *The View Painters of Europe*, trans. Pamela Waley (New York: Phaidon, 1970), esp. pp. 6–34; for Copley's specific use of existing harbor views of Havana, see Jules David Prown, *John Singleton Copley* (Cambridge, Mass.: Harvard Univ. Press, 1966), 2: 271 and figs. 368–70.

6. On Rubens as a general source, see, for example, Prown, 2: 273–75; on the link to Gericault, see Benedict Nicolson, "The 'Raft' from the Point of View of Subject Matter," *Burlington Magazine* 96 (1954): 242–43; the *Moby-Dick* reference is, of course, to Melville's great metaphysical and epistemological excursus on the sublime in "The Whiteness of the Whale," chap. 42.

7. *Letters & Papers of John Singleton Copley and Henry Pelham, 1739–1776*, [Boston:] *Massachusetts Historical Society Collections*, 71 (Boston, 1914): 236, 239–40, 245; for his practice upon his return to London, see Prown, 2: 260–64. The *Boy with a Squirrel* (a portrait of young Pelham) is reproduced in Prown, 1, fig. 163. The report of his European discoveries is amply recorded in the *Copley-Pelham Letters*, pp. 223–356 and visually recorded in his Roman double portrait of the *Izards* (1775), Prown, vol. 2, fig. 342.

8. *Copley-Pelham Letters*, pp. 241, 246, 299.

9. Sir Joshua Reynolds, *Discourses on Art*, ed. Robert R. Wark (San Marino, Calif.: Huntington Library, 1959), p. 26. This edition is cited hereinafter in the text by parenthetical page reference only. On the colonial tradition, see Neil Harris, *The Artist in American Society: The Formative Years, 1790–1860* (New York: Braziller, 1966), pp. 6–8, 56 ff.; cf. *Copley-Pelham Letters*, pp. 97–98.

10. *Copley-Pelham Letters*, pp. 41–60, 64–69, 72–73, 116, 118–19, 194–97; cf., with the last of these, Franziska Forster-Hahn, "The Sources of True Taste: Benjamin West's Instructions to a Young Painter for his Studies in Italy," *Journal of the Warburg & Courtauld Institutes* 30 (1967): 367–82.

11. In fact, the trap for the American in these words was twofold: the idea of "drapery" denied both the challenge to excell in the depiction of the pictorially and socially luxurious fabrics in which the wealthy colonial sitters of Copley or Feke or Blackburn were so splendidly arrayed *and* the emergent contrasting ideal of American social and sartorial identity as "homespun," urged by Franklin in the *Autobiography* and elsewhere, crystallized later in the "Prologue" to Royall Tyler's *The Contrast . . .* (1787):

But modern youths, with imitative sense,
Deem taste in dress the proof of excellence;
And spurn the meanness of your homespun arts,
Since homespun habits would obscure their parts;
Whilst all, which aims at splendour and parade,
Must come from Europe, and be ready made.

12. Cf. *Copley-Pelham Letters*, pp. 302–3 and Reynolds, *Discourses*, pp. 27 and 131–32, the note to which finds a more direct source for Reynolds' Lockeanism in Burke's 1759 "Introduction on Taste" to *The Sublime and Beautiful* (Boulton ed., p. 17, which in turn cites Locke, *Essay on Human Understanding* 2. 2. 2; 2. 12. 2).

The philosophical dominion which Locke exercised over eighteenth-century America is a truism of intellectual history. Thus one may speculate that when Reynolds in the *Discourses* cautioned his audience that "enthusiastic admiration seldom promotes knowledge. . . . [the student of art] examines his own mind, and perceives there nothing of that divine inspiration with which, he is told, so many others have been favored" (p. 43), his American reader was prepared to assent, not only on aesthetic or epistemological grounds but because the eighteenth-century American religious community had been taught by both Jonathan Edwards and his opponents during the Great Awakening the dangers of "enthusiasm" in Lockean cadences. (See e.g., Perry Miller, *Jonathan Edwards* [New York: William Sloane, 1949], pp. 143–44, 173–74, 178–79; and Miller, "The Rhetoric of Sensation," *Errand into the Wilderness* [Cambridge, Mass.: Harvard Univ. Press, 1956], pp. 167–83.)

13. *Copley-Pelham Letters*, p. 226. The West painting, in the National Gallery of Canada, Ottowa, is reproduced in Prown, vol. 2, fig. 366. On the significance of the *Death of Wolfe*, see below, note 16.

14. *Copley-Pelham Letters*, pp. 43–45. It should be noted that the accuracy of Reynolds' description of the course of Raphael's career is not here at issue (for his errors, see the Wark ed., *Discourses*, p. 15 n.).

15. *Copley-Pelham Letters*, pp. 245, 247, 249, 297–302, 331, 339–40; for Reynolds' frequent references to Raphael in the *Discourses*, see the excellent index in the Wark ed.

16. *Copley-Pelham Letters*, p. 340; Prown, 2: 250–55, 263–64, and figs. 340, 347. Edgar Wind, "The Revolution of History Painting," *Journal of the Warburg Institute* 2 (1938–39): 116–27, should be supplemented with Charles Mitchell, "Benjamin West's 'Death of Wolfe' and the Popular History Piece," *Journal of the Warburg & Courtauld Institutes* 7 (1944): 20–33, and Wind's corrective note, "Penny, West, and the 'Death of Wolfe,'" ibid., 10 (1947): 159–62, which is especially good on the debate between Reynolds and West.

17. *Discourses*, p. 104; or as he put it in the Fifth *Discourse:* "Raffaelle's materials are generally borrowed, though the noble structure is his own" (p. 84). The idea is, of course, an ancient one, stretching back to Plato. For

its importance to Reynolds, see Ernst Gombrich, "Reynolds's Theory and Practice of Imitation," *Burlington Magazine* 80 (1942): 40–45.

18. *Copley-Pelham Letters*, p. 299; cf. ibid., p. 296 and *Discourses*, p. 58. For a perceptive earlier view of the meaning of Copley's European experience, see Virgil Barker, *American Painting, History and Interpretation* (New York: Macmillan, 1950), pp. 212–14.

19. See Wind and Mitchell, cited above, note 16.

20. In his key letter on his *Ascension*, Copley notes that Pelham has a print after the *Laocoön* (*Copley-Pelham Letters*, p. 305); Copley bought a cast of the *Laocoön* while in Rome but it was smashed in transit to London (Prown, 2: 253). His interest in the work is not surprising since the *Laocoön* group was one of the most famous sculptures in the Vatican collection. It had been a focus of debate and discussion among artists and scholars in and beyond Rome for some time, especially since Johann Joachim Winckelmann discussed it in his early *Von der Nachahmung der griechischen Werke in der Malerei und Bildhauerkunst* (1755), quoted in the opening page of Gotthold Ephraim Lessing's famous essay of 1766: "As the depths of the sea remain always at rest, however the surface may be agitated, so the expression in the figures of the Greeks reveals in the midst of passion a great and steadfast soul . . . such a soul is depicted in the countenance of the Laocoön, under sufferings the most intense." *Laocoön: An Essay upon the Limits of Painting and Poetry*, trans. Ellen Frothingham (New York: Farrar, Straus and Giroux, Noonday Press, 1957), p. 1. Reynolds refers to it in the *Discourses*, pp. 128, 151 (there linking it with the *Gladiator*, which has been suggested, as we will see, as a source for *Watson*), 178, 180; and it was mentioned by Jonathan Richardson, Algarotti, and de Piles, whose works Copley knew in America (Prown, 1: 16).

21. The poised harpooner of the *Watson* "imitates" in a general sense innumerable versions of the St. George figure, poised with his spear over the dragon.

22. Heinrich Wölfflin, *Classic Art: An Introduction to the Italian Renaissance* (London: Phaidon, 1952), p. 135 and passim; for the Cartoons, see the reproductions in John Wyndham Pope-Hennessy, intro., *The Raphael Cartoons* (London: Victoria & Albert Museum, 1950).

23. For the division of Copley and West along the lines of the seventeenth-century battle between the Rubenistes and Poussinistes, see Prown, 2: 273–74; for the *Lion Hunt* print, ibid., vol. 2, fig. 380, which should be compared with the more frozen action—closer to Copley also in gestural details like the two figures bending out of the boat and the hand in benediction, as well as in the three bands of foreground birds, middle ground boats, and background landscape—of Raphael's *Miraculous Draught of Fishes* (*Raphael Cartoons*, fig. 1).

24. See *Prown*, 2: 273 and fig. 379.

25. Reynolds, *Discourses*, pp. 81–84, 276; Monk, *The Sublime*, pp. 167–93.

26. Prown, 2: 311–12; James Howgego, "Copley and the Corporation of London," *Guildhall Miscellany* 9 (July 1958): 34–43; Wind also explores the importance of the Americans in his "Revolution of History Painting," pp. 124–26.

27. The childhood anecdote is recounted in Amory, p. 11; the two early paintings and their print sources are reproduced in Prown, vol. 1, figs. 7–10. Of the 116 men whose occupations are listed in Prown's statistical analyses, 52 were merchants, 4 shippers, and at least one, James Gambier, a captain in the Royal Navy. Yet only four of the portraits show the boat-harbor convention which was frequently used by painters as an emblem of a merchant (and two of these are of Boylston). Gambier is depicted against a landscape! (Prown, 1: 121–22, and figs. 56, 182, 184, 220, 325.) For a survey of colonial seascape portraiture, see John Wilmerding, *A History of American Marine Painting* (Salem & Boston: Peabody Museum/Little, Brown, 1968), chap. 1.

28. Family tradition had it that he heard the story from Watson himself because the two travelled to England together in 1774; it now seems more likely that he heard it from his own brother-in-law who had sailed with Watson two years later. (See the information supplied in the entry on the 1778 Boston Museum of Fine Arts replica, almost identical to the original version in the National Gallery of Art: *American Paintings in the Museum of Fine Arts, Boston* [Boston, 1969], 1: 81.)

29. The practical inhibitions to pictorial art in the colonies were great—and obvious—and the resulting efforts at pictorial seascape are correspondingly sparse, though they do exist, even in the seventeenth century. Wilmerding's summary (see note 27 above) is by no means exhaustive. By the end of the colonial period there existed prints and other graphics, fireboards, wall paintings and papers, sketches, harborscapes, and even, in 1772, William Williams' small *Imaginary Landscape* (a harbor scene, in the Newark Museum), as well as occasional sculptural uses. Limitations of space forbid their inclusion in this discussion, though they all help to create a context for Copley's *Watson*. See Roger B. Stein, *Seascape and the American Imagination* (New York: Clarkson Potter/Whitney Museum of American Art, 1975).

30. See Roger B. Stein, "Seascape and the American Imagination; The Puritan Seventeenth Century," *Early American Literature* 7 (Spring 1972): 17–37.

31. Cotton Mather, *Magnalia Christi Americana: Or, The Ecclesiastical History of New England*, ed. Rev. Thomas Robbins (Hartford, S. Andrus & Son, 1853), 2: 342, 343, cited hereinafter in the text by parenthetical page reference only. The literature on Fortuna is large and impressive; for useful background to Mather, see Howard R. Patch, *The Goddess Fortuna in Mediaeval Literature* (Cambridge, Mass.: Harvard Univ. Press, 1927).

32. Publius Vergilius Maro *Aeneid* 3.191: "vela damus vastumque cava trabe currimus aequor" (Loeb Classical Library ed.).

33. Wind, "Revolution of History Painting," pp. 119, 121–23.

34. Copley's interest in the work, as he talks of it in his letter to Pelham, centers on the lower range (*Copley-Pelham Letters*, pp. 297–98); by contrast, Wölfflin sees a logical development in Raphael from the *Heliodorus* to the *Transfiguration* in his ability to integrate upper and lower ranges of the canvas (*Classic Art*, p. 137).

35. The domination of vast space in nineteenth-century America is a commonplace, both in terms of land—as Frederick Jackson Turner made theoretically clear—and in terms of sea—as Melville and Mahan indicate. Its religious dimension, its connection with the sublime generally, and in some cases with God in particular, has also been noted. Perhaps its most articulate spokesman was Fenimore Cooper, one of whose characters speaks of "the immensity of moral space which separates man from his Deity" (*The Sea Lions* [Lincoln: Univ. of Nebraska Press, 1965], p. 274; see also Donald A. Ringe, *The Pictorial Mode: Space and Time in the Art of Bryant, Irving and Cooper* [Lexington: Univ. Press of Kentucky, 1971]).

36. *American Tradition in Painting* (New York: Braziller, 1963), pp. 19–20.

37. A powerful horizontal orientation would continue to be a dominant quality of American art of the next hundred years, as many have noted. Curiously, Copley's one significant addition to his print source in the 1754 oil copy of *The Return of Neptune* was a horizon line—as if Americans learned that lesson almost at birth (see Prown, vol. 1, figs. 9–10).

38. Herman Melville, *Moby-Dick*, chap. 119.

39. West's explorations in the sublime mode were mostly explicitly religious. His first, *Saul and the Witch of Endor*, was done one year before the *Watson*. The first version of *Death on a Pale Horse* is about 1783. See Grose Evans, *Benjamin West and the Taste of His Times* (Carbondale: Southern Illinois Univ. Press, 1959), pp. 55–81.

40. Taylor's Meditations 2:29 and 2:30 are discussed in Stein, "Seascape," pp. 28–30; the relation of the novel to Bunyan and its implications for American fiction are discussed in J. Paul Hunter, *The Reluctant Pilgrim: Defoe's Emblematic Quest for Form in "Robinson Crusoe"* (Baltimore: Johns Hopkins Univ. Press, 1966); for Williams and the tangled history of *Mr. Penrose* see David Howard Dickason, *William Williams: Novelist and Painter of Colonial America, 1727–1791* (Bloomington: Indiana Univ. Press, 1970) and Dickason's edition of the original MS of *Mr. Penrose: The Journal of Penrose, Seaman* (Bloomington: Indiana Univ. Press, 1969); for a discussion of eighteenth-century American sea fiction in general, see Roger B. Stein, "Pulled Out of the Bay: American Fiction in the Eighteenth Century," *Studies in American Fiction* 2 (Spring 1974): 13–36.

41. *The Works of the Right Honorable Edmund Burke*, 3d. ed. (Boston: Little, Brown, 1869), 2: 117.

42. Ibid., 2: 117–18.

43. These five letters, 4–8, were probably written between 1769 and 1774, before the opening of the war, and at a time when Crevecoeur was also composing impressionistic travel sketches of Lisbon, Jamaica, Bermuda, and the Southern colonies, according to Thomas Philbrick (*St. John de Crevecoeur* [New York: Twayne, 1970], p. 20). Letter 1, which refers to "friend Edmund, whose speeches I often see in our papers" (p. 42), was written later but makes it clear that Crevecoeur knew of Burke's formulation before he submitted his own final copy to the printer. The page ref. here and in the text below is to the Signet Classics ed. of the *Letters . . . and Sketches* (New York, 1963).

44. It matters not, in this connection, that in fact the scene takes place within Havana harbor, since the viewer's conscious experience is not of a land world behind him but of waves lapping perilously close to him at the lower edge of the canvas.

45. Elayne A. Rapping, "Theory and Experience in Crevecoeur's America," *American Quarterly* 19 (Winter 1967): 707–15.

46. *Second Treatise on Government*, chap. 5, par. 49. Burke explored the Crusoe-type of image in his speech on taxation in the colonies, 19 April 1774, when he described the colonial venture as "a set of miserable outcasts a few years ago, not so much sent as thrown out on the bleak and barren shore of a desolate wilderness three thousand miles from all civilized intercourse" (*Works*, 2: 33). If fact could be used as source material for fiction, so fiction could be used to reinforce and give symbolic weight to fact; the reciprocity of relationship is crucial to an understanding of the significance of American seascape.

47. As it turned out, Brook Watson was later to support in Parliament the continuation of the slave trade, which brought down on him—and Copley's picture—the wrath of a later historian of art: William Dunlap, *History of the Rise and Progress of the Arts of Design in the United States* (1834; rpt. of 1918 ed., New York: B. Blom, 1965), 1: 133–34.

48. Prown, 2: 273–74, treats the problem solely as one of sources and composition; Wind, "Revolution," p. 119, as exotica; see also Mitchell, p. 21 and n.

49. Although the full discussion of this issue deserves and will receive separate treatment, I can at least suggest here the historical context within which the black in *Watson* needs to be seen. The 1770s was a period of intense anti-slavery agitation in Britain, focusing in part on the closing of the slave trade to the West Indies, in part on manumission. Given the Havana setting of *Watson* and the benedictory gesture of the black, one needs to consider both the political discussions about the slave trade, in Parliament and in the press, and the group of slave autobiographies being published in London, many of which are in effect conversion narratives with substantial sections of sea adventures. (Joshua Reynolds was on the

subscription list of at least one of these.) See, as a beginning, C. Duncan Rice, *The Rise and Fall of Black Slavery* (New York: Harper & Row, 1974); Angelo Costanzo, "The Art and Tradition of Black Autobiography in the Eighteenth Century" (unpublished Ph.D. dissertation, State University of New York at Binghamton, 1976).

THEATRE VERSUS DRAMA: POPULAR

ENTERTAINMENT IN EARLY AMERICA

A study of American social history or politics, or indeed almost any other study purporting to portray American historical life, would find its reflection in drama. "If," said Tocqueville, "you would judge beforehand of the literature of a people that is lapsing into democracy, study its dramatic productions." [1] It has become standard to say that the drama has traditionally served as the middle ground between the great, moving ideas of an age and their popular acceptance, and one would thus expect great excitement about early American plays, yet American drama is often ignored. The early plays tend to be regarded as separate phenomena, as if such plays were isolated from other aspects of American life and culture rather than being real social occasions and reflections of the dreams, aspirations, and ideas of a people. Most often the plays are looked upon with contempt (when looked upon at all) and are rarely included in any study of the period.

In part this attitude derives from the attitudes of the original audiences themselves. A sort of snobbery pervaded the theatre, and the assumption, at least on the East Coast, was that American dramatists were somehow inferior to European. Economic forces helped to shape this point of view, since most managers would rather steal a European play than pay royalties on an American one. Ambrose Bierce's definition of a dramatist as "one who adapts plays from the French" was not entirely inaccurate. Yet American plays were turned out in surprising profusion, and there is much meat in them, and much to aid our understanding of cultural history.

These early American plays are dismissed for another, more essentially literary reason: how does one equate *Hamlet* with *Mucedorus*, Ibsen with Boucicault? The plays of Foote were as popular as those of Shakespeare in the eighteenth century, and in the nineteenth, Boucicault was referred to as the Shakespeare of his day. *Literary* critics pass judgments on contemporary plays with the whole canon behind them, while *theatre* critics, by nature more sympathetic to each new play as it is performed, tend to stay in the theatre, finding little time or inclination to write down their thoughts in journalistic form. And for literary critics, eighteenth- and nineteenth-century American drama was dry ground: a huge number of intellectually inferior plays, and no great dramatists.

Many people of all classes went to the theatre, and theatrical entertainment opened the frontier almost as fast as pioneers did, and, further, there were great theatrical changes (the star system combined with the stock company, new kinds of stage effects, and the like). But the criteria retained to evaluate what showed up on American stages were almost entirely *literary*, and *theatre* criticism was found wanting: witness Washington Irving's 1807 censure of contemporary critics: "Having never seen Kemble in this character," he wrote, "we are absolutely at a loss to say whether Mr. Cooper played it well or not." [2] When inspected at all, American plays were viewed as novels for the stage, and depth of characterization, plausibility and tautness of plot, symbols, poetic language—all literary criteria—were used to evaluate our drama.

Yet it is frequently in non-literary ways that the drama makes itself felt—in music, in the ephemeral appeal of one event, in a mood, perhaps in one actor. Thus, there must be aesthetic criteria beyond the merely literary. We need an explanation of why Dion Boucicault's *Octoroon*, for example, was able to play in the North and South, despite its theme; why the building of its internal forces toward the auction scene resulted in a theatrical statement trite to recount yet so powerful as to capture audiences then and now in the playhouse.

The appreciation and the evaluation of our early drama must come from an inspection of its role as a mirror of our culture, and must consider the *American theatre*, not *dramatic literature*. The relation between art and culture must be the basis of our critical evaluation. If the nineteenth-century American theatre found itself with a heterogeneous audience, one largely untrained in the formal Continental tradition, and if the drama's response was to stress native elements, then we must come to terms with those popular elements. After all, our folk heroes, for example, showed up first on stage. If the riverboatman, the Yankee, the plantation Negro, the cowboy are inarticulate yet biting, naive yet shrewd, and if their drama reveals them, then it reveals something distinctly American. The lower classes found themselves on stage (even as the English middle class earlier found its dramatic image in works like Lillo's *London Merchant*) with an orientation uncluttered by any traditional European approach. The stage became less strictly verbal, and if the result was not the *Gesamtkunstwerk* sought by Wagner, it did take greater advantage of music, lighting, painting, machinery, in a new democratic drama.

Perhaps the best way to draw these threads together is to inspect three dramatic forms, the three which were most popular in nineteenth-century America, which served both as transition between the nation's dramatic origins and its current theatre and which, in addition, best serve to illustrate America's distinctly "popular" drama.

In the eighteenth century America emulated every British form at least once: tragedy (*Prince of Parthia*), comedy of manners (*The Contrast*), ballad opera (*The Disappointment*), comic opera (*The Archers*), and every British trend (as in adaptations from the French and German). In the nineteenth century, American audiences viewed a great proliferation of dramatic forms, though only three forms made their way from the eighteenth century to the twentieth with steady popularity.

Our first consideration, the comic or English opera, was a play with many songs. The songs might illustrate the action, push it forward, or even be appropriate to it—as later music critics desired—but they might not, and there is no evidence that the integration of music and drama had anything to do with the form's popularity. One of the best-known English writers of comic opera, William Dimond, said of English opera's rules:

> In its *Plot*, it may be either serious or sprightly, or it may combine both qualities, *ad libitum*, with just a sufficient interest to excite attention and to banish *ennui* during the necessary spaces between song and song, but never so vividly to stimulate the feelings of an Audience, as to make the recurrence of Music be felt as an impertinent interruption. . . . Above all, the MUSICAL SITUATIONS ought to spring with spontaneity out of the very necessities of the Scene; never betraying themselves to be labored introductions for the mere purpose of exhibiting vocal talent, but always to appear so many integral portions and indispensable continuations of the story.[3]

His criteria are excellent, and one day they might form the basis for a closely knit American musical comedy. But not in the nineteenth century.

Language itself was slighted in the comic opera. With the possible exception of political oratory—a kind of entertainment in some sections of the country—Americans tended (and tend) to mistrust speech. Elaborate speech on stage might in-

dicate foreign influence and was in any case suspect, except
in the conventional speech of melodrama. Our inarticulate
folk heroes needed some different element on stage in order
to communicate, and music provided that element, a means of
conveying ideas other than through speech, a means of adding
to the play a quality lost as reliance on words alone disap-
peared.

The ancestor of comic opera, ballad opera, showed up in
America early in the eighteenth century. *Flora, or Hob in the
Well,* for example, was performed in Charleston in 1735 and
The Beggar's Opera probably had more performances than
any other work on American stages in the eighteenth century.
The form used old music set to new words, music subordinate
to plot, spoken dialogue, a comic plot. Another manifestation
of the comic opera was the *pasticcio,* where music (not bal-
lads) was stolen from the best sources; from here it was an
easy jump to full comic opera, where all the music was composed especially for the work. These comic operas were called
English opera in the nineteenth century, largely to separate
them in everyone's mind from real, or grand, or Italian opera.
They were in the forefront of the repertory, so that as theatre
traveled in America—to Cincinnati, Albany, Pittsburgh, Gal-
veston, Washoe, Seattle, and San Francisco—it was largely a
musical theatre. The point cannot be stressed too heavily.
Where England could absorb the musical trend into a cen-
turies-old tradition of drama, here there was no other tradition, and the musical stage, in one form or another, became
America's only theatre. The argument may be made by anal-
ogy. Louis Hartz [4] has pointed out that John Locke was subject to a kind of Americanizing experience: he became America's *only* theoretical tradition in politics and, because America
had no clearly established elite and was not part of the European struggle against a feudal aristocracy, Locke assumed a
significance here he never had in England. So, too, with the
musical stage; imported as the most popular current English

stage form, it lost the place it had in England as merely one part of a venerable tradition and became something else: America's standard, traditional, and most widely accepted stage form. Like the tradition itself, its form, its content, and its influence underwent a sea change. Even when the very nature of American performances (that is, a resident stock company greeting either stars or some sort of specialty troupes) shattered the known repertory and forced variety on the stage, the variety which was welcomed was most frequently musical. For example, the Ravel troupe was one of the most popular "star" visitors all over the country, yet they put on short musical plays and dances, and even their acrobatics were primarily in the service of elaborate pantomimes.

These musicals in the repertory also afforded form, content, and training to America's developing drama. The need to support any visiting star forced stock companies into great versatility. If Mlle. Celeste came by with a bill of dances, the stock company danced. If the Sequin Opera Company (composed of four singers[5]) came with the *Bohemian Girl* or *Guy Mannering* or *La Sonnambula*, the stock company was forced to do a good bit of singing. This was no great change from the eighteenth century, when actors' contracts specified two types of role: straight dramatic and singing. Yet something of the versatility of these nineteenth-century actors may be seen in Clara Fisher, for example ("In her earlier years," said George Willard,[6] "her success was equally apparent in tragedy, opera, or farce, but later in life her face, voice, and person were best adapted to the lighter characters of opera and comedy"), or Lydia Kelly, who played Beatrice in *Much Ado About Nothing*, Rosalind in *As You Like It*, Ophelia in *Hamlet*, and sang Susannah in *The Marriage of Figaro* and Bertha in *Der Freischütz*.[7] If the twentieth-century American musical comedy actor amazes audiences abroad with his ability to dance, sing, and act, the basis for his training was achieved in the stock companies on our nineteenth-century stages.

If all performers sang and danced, so all comic operas written in America reflected certain national elements in their
form and content. The form tended always to shift toward
burlesque and parody, so that one constantly finds an attempt
at comic opera followed by laughter at the attempt, or an
English opera burlesqued by an American version (for example, *Zampa, the Red Corsair* managed to emerge as *Sam
Parr and His Red Coarse Hair*). Burlesque, with its exaggerated style, was an echo not only of the pervasive melodrama but of America's insistence on laughing at itself (a
privilege it did not extend, as Mrs. Trollope and other visitors
discovered, to others). Surely the absurdity of the burlesque,
the flouting of logic, was an extension of the desire to flout
all authority. Pretentiousness needed to be exploded, but so
did good manners in a period fast approaching Jackson, and
the musical was the best theatrical explosive available. And if
the first quarter of the nineteenth century saw a good many
American musicals being written (*The Forest Rose, The Saw-
Mill, The Indian Princess*), it also saw the content of these
musicals beginning to reflect the American experience. Democratic communities, said Tocqueville "want to hear something
that concerns themselves, and the delineation of the present
age is what they demand." [8] The melodeon farces so popular
in California used local themes and coloring, for example, such
as *The Last Chance in Virginia City, or the Speculator and
his Jackass.*[9] If *Lola Montes in Bavaria* was a hit, then the
burlesque of the musical quickly followed: *Who's Got the
Countess.*[10] Contemporary events, local and national, showed
up immediately on America's stages.[11] Comic opera, with local
characters and situations, provided parts that could not easily
be acted by foreign actors, and so drama and acting developed
hand in hand.

The songs of the comic operas (and, later, of the minstrel
shows) were also significant. As late as the Civil War, "It was
in the songs more than in the plays that the patriotic feeling

of the times found expression in the theatre." [12] A flood of songs recorded the development of the nation. A good example is William Dunlap's *Yankee Chronology: Or, Huzzah for the Constitution*.[13] He wrote the piece as an interlude, a musical one, to help celebrate the Fourth of July 1812 in the theatre. The growth of his musical clearly shows the relationship between the stage and current events. He added a stanza celebrating one of the naval victories of the War of 1812, and then, on request, to celebrate the anniversary of the year the British left New York he added still another; when, in February 1813, the U.S. *Constitution* seized the British frigate, *Java*, he added still more, the gist of which can be gathered from such lines as ". . . sailors fight best when they fight to be free." Fashions and politics, then, were good matter for musicals.[14] The entire theme of J.N.B. Barker's *Indian Princess* (1808) is summarized in its final song. Though plot elements are tied together in individual stanzas, the reprise (sung three times) makes the point clear:

> Freedom, on the western shore
>   Float thy banner o'er the brave;
> Plenty, here thy blessings pour;
>   Peace, thy olive sceptre wave! [15]

In addition to the popularity of comic opera, grand opera made a deep impression on the American theatre. At the beginning, almost no distinction was made between the two genres. When Signorina Garcia (later Mme. Malibran) left New York in the 1827–28 season, her farewell performances included both types: *The Barber of Seville, The Devil's Bridge, Love in a Village*, and *Don Giovanni*. Visiting troupes came by with both types of opera, and stock companies were expected to handle both in addition to their regular chores. Such an astute scholar as Odell, however, lost the forest in the musical trees: "We never cease to marvel, in these early bills, at such unions of the operatic and the dramatic. . . ." And when Helene, the Italian Troubadour who played five instruments at once, departed the New York stage, Odell heaved a sigh and said ". . . how one longs for the day when variety halls will drain off such atrocities from the regular playhouses!" [16] The point is that the atrocities which bothered him, the union of the musical and the dramatic which offended his sensibilities, never did leave the stage. To be sure, later in the century grand opera did manage to achieve a certain snob value and did manage to split off from the musical in terms of its audience appeal, though not as a form: it had always been different there. See Philip Hone's description of grand opera's function in 1846:

> This opera of ours [i.e., the new Italian opera house at Astor Place] is a refined amusement, creditable to the taste of its proprietors and patrons; a beautiful parterre in which our young ladies, the flowers of New York society, are planted to expand in a congenial soil, under the sunshine of admiration; and here also our young men may be initiated into the habits and forms of elegant social intercourse, and learn to acquire a taste for a science of the most refined and elegant nature. . . .[17]

When one compares this sort of ideal with the behavior observed by Mrs. Trollope in the American theatre (smoking, spitting, hats on, legs over rails), one sees grand opera becoming a cultivated art even as our musical stage, that of the comic opera, becomes a popular one. Observe *The Saw-Mill* (1824): [18] a comic servant steps on stage before a word of dialogue has been spoken, and in his easy relation to his master, in his casual treatment of social forms, in his singing what might in another age and another country be spoken, he stands, almost all by himself, for what was happening in one of the American theatre's most popular early forms.

The second form popular on our early stages was melodrama, though the line between it and comic opera was sometimes a fuzzy one. *The Indian Princess*, referred to earlier, was called on its title page "an operatic melo-drame." Still, the

basic type was clear, and melodrama was another mold, not in-
digneous, yet nonetheless one into which America poured new
ideas and one which reflects American culture. Yet there is
an important difference between the comic opera and melodrama. While comic opera might be traced in various countries to a long past, such as ballad opera in England (or even
the Elizabethan jig) or *opera buffa* in Italy or *singspiel* in Germany, the melodrama was a relatively new form, whatever its
roots, by the time it arrived in America. August von Kotzebue
(1761–1819) wrote, after all, in the late eighteenth century,
and his popularity swept Germany, France, and England. His
chaste women, his insistence that learning is not necessary to
the man of pure heart, these went a long way toward form-
ing the themes of melodrama. In fact, the majority of German
plays acted in America in the late 1700s were Dunlap adaptations of the works of Kotzebue with—as befits a precursor of
melodrama—music by some of America's outstanding composers.[19] And shortly thereafter melodrama made its formal
debut in England and in France.

Though the term *melodrame* had been recorded earlier, and
indeed for a while was used as a synonym for opera in general, the new form and the term came together in the works
of Guilbert de Pixérécourt, and melodrama was launched from
both sides of the English Channel almost simultaneously in the
latter 1790s. Pixérécourt wrote more than fifty melodramas,
his most successful being *Coelina* in 1800; it was translated by
Holcroft as the *Tale of Mystery* in 1802 and first shown in
America in 1803. Pixérécourt established as a definite dramatic
type what had been a hybrid form of entertainment, "an
exaggerated story interspersed with music, dances, and acrobatics." [20] He introduced rules and conventions, and his unique
contribution was to weld the *scène lyrique* with pantomime
entertainment and the atmosphere and techniques of the English Gothic school. Other elements of the melodrama had
been popular on America's eighteenth-century stages, both in

the serious "speaking pantomimes" and in the use of Gothic elements. Add to all these the fact that all American playhouses had a theatre band, and we were ready to start.

Melodrama began its development in America at approximately the same time it began elsewhere, carrying with it some elements, such as stock characters. One always saw, in the beginning, the pure, chaste heroine (M. Wilson Disher saw a "cosmic partiality for the virginal" [21]), the villain, the hero, the old father, the comic servants. Sharp contrasts in morality, whirlwind action, spectacular stage effects—these too were standard. One other element was crucial for early melodrama: its music. It is a mistake to think of music as subordinate in melodrama; the form itself was largely derived from earlier musical genres, and one must look to the music to understand melodrama's effect not only on the nineteenth-century opera (e.g., the convention of certain instruments being identified with certain characters or certain situations) but on the ultimate shape of the form as it dominated America's stages in the nineteenth century. True, there were many songs in melodrama, but it was not the songs which made the shape of the entertainment as much as it was the music which set off entrances, scenes of special emotion, elaborate stage effects. Music permitted actors to pantomime much of their roles, indeed forced them to, and a new acting style evolved for melodrama as a result. Add to all of these music for melodrama's dances and pageants and the like, and it becomes increasingly difficult to tell a melodrama from a musical comedy. In fact, it was Allardyce Nicoll who noted how fine the line is, in an age of melodrama and of musical comedy, between the purely dramatic and the purely operatic.[22]

Again, the nature of America's stock companies in the nineteenth century helped melodrama gain and retain its popularity. Actors' contracts called for a particular type of role, and no doubt plays were selected which could be cast from among the stock characters available in a company. A quick glance at some of the actors in Caldwell's New Orleans company in 1821 shows how easily the standard stock company parts would fit into melodrama as the latter became more and more popular:

> Mr. James H. Caldwell, manager, and leading actor in tragedy and comedy. . . . N. M. Ludlow, juvenile tragedy and first genteel comedy, when not played by the manager; Richard Russell, stage-manager and low-comedy actor; Thomas Burke, first old men and a portion of low comedy. . . . Jackson Gray, principal old men in some instances, and second in others. . . . Mrs. Cornelia Burke, principal singer and first comedy 'romps'. . . . Miss Eliza Tilden . . . juvenile tragedy and sentimental comedy lady. . . .[23]

There is no doubt of melodrama's popularity in America. It was played wherever there was a troupe to act: aboard show boats, even with minstrel companies, in sophisticated cities and newly opened territories. David Grimsted's study of its place in the repertory by 1850 shows that in Charleston it made up 32 percent of the repertory, in Philadelphia 52 percent, and in New Orleans and St. Louis 50 percent.[24]

From a literary point of view, melodramas were a disaster; the characters were neither psychologically sound (except as they revealed something of the audiences who loved them) nor did they have the supposed purgative effect of humors characters. Plots were unimportant, since they were immutable and rigidly patterned, not after a moral ritual but after a poetic justice outside morality. And both plot and character were couched in a language containing neither reality nor poetry.

What, then, was there in the form and content of melodrama to make such an appeal? And how did melodrama reflect the society on which it made its impress? I have already suggested the relationship between the stock company and melodramatic acting. Add to this melodrama's willingness to absorb those novelties of which nineteenth-century American audiences were so fond: circus acts and horse operas (e.g., *Mazeppa*), plus the delight Americans found in laughing at pretension, which resulted in the paradox of popular melodramas immediately followed by popular burlesques of the very same works. (A Boston production of *Undine; or, the Spirit of the Water*, for instance, was followed a few nights later at a rival house by *Undone! or, Spirits and Water* [25].) In the melodrama, it is tempting (and presumptuous) to discuss at length the American's change from the ideals of reason (perhaps best exemplified in Dunlap's goals for the stage) or abstract ideas generally, to a romantic view of the good American as an intuitive product of nature (Mrs. Mowatt's *Fashion* illustrates the point) with specific, emotion-charged symbols (the log cabin), to the kind of pessimism (realism, if you will) that even Boucicault's stage version of *Rip Van Winkle* suggests.[26] These ideas are in the melodramas of the period, ideas suited to a form that idealized the very contrasts lived by men along the frontier. Acting styles developed from such plays, and an industrial society's best inventions were used and admired on the stage, such as the spurious realism of a real train giving the illusion of crushing the heroine. Melodrama gave the illusion of life, the illusion of a reality already lost, the memory of a dream, and it is no wonder that melodrama took its place at the forefront of the American stage.

The third popular form on the early stage was our only indigenous one, the minstrel show. Here, too, form and content flout literary drama's rules and also reflect American society for nearly half a century. Elements of the form can be traced back in time to other countries (blackfacing a white man, for example) and other elements can be traced to American features (such as identification of the Negro slave with song and with dance), but these are scholarly games, not especially relevant to the subject. Relevance comes when Thomas Dartmouth Rice, a competent actor, introduced a song and dance into a play in which he was appearing as a Kentucky cornfield

Negro in 1829 or 1830. It was a number he had picked up from watching a crippled Negro; Rice performed the song in tattered clothes and used Negro dialect. The chorus, repeated between verses, ran:

> So I wheel about,
> I turn about,
> I do just so,
> And ebery time I wheel about,
> I jump Jim Crow.

"Jim Crow" Rice's imitation (an excellent one, from contemporary accounts) of a Southern plantation Negro went all over the country as inter-act entertainment. Other performers imitated the character, some even using the same name. An outstanding folklore character was born. The Southern plantation Negro was happy, comical, naive, shrewd, boastful— was, in fact, beneath his burnt cork, a Yankee, a river boatman, an urban fireman. (I might add that he was not a slave, though he stood for a justification of slavery.)

Rice then took the next step. He incorporated his newly created character (newly discovered is perhaps better) in a series of "extravaganzas," or ballad operas with dialogue, song, and dance. His *Bone Squash, Oh! Hush!*, and the like were added to the bills at various theatres, where one might find a Shakespeare play, Rice performing "Jim Crow," and an "Ethiopian Opera" all on the same bill.

A further step, a gathering of Negro entertainment (that is, an imitation of Negro entertainment) popular at the time, such as dancers, banjo players, and singers in one bill, was taken by E. P. Christy, and the final step, consolidation of elements into a new form, by Daniel Decatur Emmett.[27] In 1843, in blackface, Emmett (who had been an entertainer, especially in the circus, for years) playing the violin, Frank Bower (who already had a reputation as a comedian, singer, and bone player) playing the bones, Bill Whitlock on the banjo, and Dick Pelham on the tambourine, made their debut in New York as the Virginia Minstrels. They played, sang, and danced; they included comic bits and those extravaganzas already made popular by Rice. Again we have musical entertainment, with the ground so well prepared by other popular stage forms. Again we have comic actors singing and playing. Though the form developed, changed, nonetheless the pattern had been set, a pattern which led all other theatrical forms in popularity in America for almost half a century.

A study of playbills reveals some of the more interesting changes in form and content. During the 1840s a two-part program emerged, the first showing the Northern dandy (complete with long-tailed blue coat), and the second the Southern plantation Negro. The "walkaround," usually at the end of the first part, permitted each member of the company to display his specialty numbers.

In the '50s the company grew, added other instruments, more specialty numbers, and became a three-part entertainment: In Part 1, those sentimental songs which produced some of America's finest lyrical outbursts by some of her finest composers; in Part 2, a variety of songs, dances, specialty numbers, monologues, and the like—a veritable vaudeville show, or at least the origins of *that* species of entertainment; Part 3 retained genuine Negro characteristics.

The 1860s saw the minstrel show begin to expand even further. The unpretentious little group that had traveled the frontier (and still did, where there was a frontier) now entered a town with a huge parade, gave brass band concerts outside the theatre and orchestral selections inside, and featured burlesques of grand opera as a regular part of its entertainment. In fact, many troupes were called "minstrel and burlesque opera" companies. And here again we see the sort of American irreverence toward sacred cows implied in burlesque, whether the drama, the melodrama, or the opera was being parodied. The minstrel version of *Lucia di Lammamoor*, which emerged as *Lucy Did Lam Her Moor*, is a notable example.

Minstrel shows remained popular, North and South, during

the Civil War, and after the '6os the quest for novelties sig-
naled the decline of the "Ethiopian business." The troupes
grew larger and larger, huge companies of seventy five and
one hundred grew too cumbrous to tour, and the nature of
the show underwent a change as wooden minstrels and albino
minstrels and female minstrels competed for audiences. A play-
bill for Madame Rentz's Female Minstrels in 1871 clearly
shows the decline. Three men are named as Bones, Inter-
locutor, and Tambo, and then the program lists an introductory Overture by the female minstrels, an operatic chorus, a
ballad, a comic refrain, three songs, a finale, a violin solo,
operatic selections, a jig, a banjo solo with Indian Club
Exercises, a monologue on "Congressional Efforts," two skits
followed by a "Laughable Negro Act" with three characters,
a fancy dance, John E. Taylor as the "Black Apollo," and a
"Grand Terpsichorean Carnival." The Yankee was now selling shows instead of merely acting in them.

Yet in their heyday, minstrel shows were the first forms of
entertainment to be seen all over the United States. They were
a part of circuses, they traveled on show boats, they were featured in museums. There is no doubt that part of their popularity arose from their apology for slavery—the Negro in
these shows was obviously happy, carefree, and not terribly
bright. But other elements need to be stressed if the inter-
action of minstrel shows with American culture is to be understood. For one thing, they were a "chaste" form of entertainment, musical, not likely to offend one's morals. And they
were supposed to be educational: one of their strongest appeals was authenticity. Rice's assertion in song that he danced
accurately—

> This is the style of Alabama,
>   What dey hab in Mobile,
> And dis is Louisiana,
>   Whaar dey track upon de heel—

was imitated by Christy's insistence that in the walkaround he "had always confined myself to the habit and crude ideas of the slaves of the South." [28] The pattern of "authenticity" is extended by the observation of a visitor to America that Sanford "is careful in his discrimination of the blacks of different states." [29] Even the names of the early companies—the Georgia Minstrels, the Florida Minstrels, the Kentucky Minstrels— reflected their pledge to emulate authentically the dress, habits, speech, song, and dance of Negroes in various regions of the United States. Some actual Negroes (e.g., Juba of Long Island) reached the stage and helped preserve genuine regional differences of song and dance. The influence of Negro spirituals, work songs, and camp meetings helped song writers with an idiom, a beat, and such distinctively American works as those by Stephen Foster emerged from the minstrel show's early determination to preserve its sources accurately.

Parts for American actors, a stage for writers, and an audience for composers were all provided by the minstrel show. A folk hero emerged, the plantation Negro, and if he was sad and longed for the old folks at home, maybe here, too, was an America growing up and longing for the simple ideals, the agrarian way of life, already slipping away.

What, then, do comic opera, melodrama, and the minstrel show reveal about early America and about our early drama? The serious drama moved from eighteenth-century Tyler and Dunlap abstractions concerning morality and patriotism and education toward the Jacksonian concern with something else. Nature's noblemen show up as melodramatic heroes (and actors, Edwin Forrest, e.g.) and, on a somewhat lower level, folk types show up with shrewdness and naiveté. One recent writer finds in the 1840s "a shift from speculative, rational, idea-centered intellectual thinking in our political life to a practical, emotional, object-centered thinking." [30] Arthur Hobson Quinn insists that democracy was the dominant political note from 1825 to 1840—reflected in plays of the period—not a narrow political note but "sympathy with those who opposed political oppression."[31] Another view is found in Montrose Moses' observation of realism in the drama as the "American background."[32] The idea is supported by others:

> Realism was the greatest tendency in the nineteenth century. Although in its literal meaning the term can be applied to the art of any period, it was not until the nineteenth century that realism was first used to designate both a philosophy and a style of art. Belief in the objective reality of the external world and the scientific revolution to which it is closely related brought about an equally important revolution in society, the arts in general, and the theatre in particular.[33]

And yet the drama itself and the theatre in which it plays, both end by belying the trend in America. Yes, realistic staging, but always of unbelievable situations. And if both Van Rough and Jonathan in *The Contrast* kept their eye on the main chance, there was Colonel Manly to remind them where their duty lay. The split became worse, if anything, by the 1840s, when melodrama and comic opera permitted the hero to inherit a fortune, even as the plantation Negro and the comic underplots showed that shrewdness wins out, especially over cultivation. Melodrama needed a stilted language of its own precisely to show its split from realism. The American deluded ("idealized," he might have said) himself with either high-sounding, impossible characters and language, or low-sounding sons and daughters of nature living the kind of life already disappearing.

The forms seem to interlock on all levels. The American folk heroes are said to be easy imitations of some stock comic types, for example the stage Irishman popular in the early nineteenth century. Yet when Dion Boucicault had lived in America a couple of years and studied the types in use here, he then created a stage Irishman acceptable in Ireland for the first time.[34] I suggest that imitation goes the other way around, and that the Yankee, the ethnic types, the plantation Negroes, in their simple, shrewd, sympathetic characters, with whatever Roman roots, were a new birth in early American drama. They were reflections of an ideal. Men could come to America, from any social stratum, and here, in a natural environment (the evil city is one of our oldest legends), be taught by shucking off evil ways and learning from their hearts and from the good examples set by unspoiled nature. The paradox remains: one must always learn and be moral in situations outside both learning and morality. Furthermore, the ideal of these simple characters was not only a natural one but a democratic one: all men created equal in God's eyes, capable equally of governing and making a million. Naive, shrewd, simple, complex, natural, civilized, independent, democratic— a new character creation. But beyond characters, the very mixture of forms, so abhorrent to the literary critic, provided on the stage a melange of entertainment, demanding a wide assortment of skills from the actor, and catering to an undifferentiated, democratic audience. The language was stilted and down-to-earth, for American aspiration and reality, and somehow it blended and worked. The situations were serious and comic, and they, too, worked. A country with no clear idea of itself found, somehow, a picture; not merely an escape but a picture of itself. Still another student of our drama said, ". . . out of the bastard form of native comedy, a native tradition emerges in character, in wit and humor, and . . . in dramatic structure and theme." [35] And if the result was not great American literature, it was exciting drama and good theatre.

JULIAN MATES
C. W. POST COLLEGE,
LONG ISLAND UNIVERSITY

Notes

1. Alexis de Tocqueville, *Democracy in America*, Henry Reeve text as revised by Francis Bowen, further corrected and edited by Phillips Bradley.

Originally published in 1835 and 1840 (New York: Vintage Books, 1954), 2: 84.

2. William Irving, James Kirke Paulding and Washington Irving, *Salmagundi or the Whimwhams and Opinions of Launcelot Langstaff, Esq., and Others*, 1860 (New York: G. P. Putnam's Sons, 1881), author's revised ed., from issue number 1, Saturday, 24 June 1807, p. 24.

3. William Dimond, Preface to *Native land: Or, the Return from Slavery: An Opera, in Three Acts*. (Printed for R. S. Kirby, 20, Warwick-lane, Paternoster-row, 1824), p. vi.

4. Louis Hartz, *The Liberal Tradition in America* (New York: Harcourt, Brace and Co., 1955), pp. 60–62.

5. Noah Miller Ludlow, *Dramatic Life as I Found It* . . . (1880; rpt. New York: B. Blom, 1966), p. 612.

6. George Owen Willard, *History of the Providence Stage, 1762–1891* (Providence: The Rhode Island News Co., 1891), p. 101.

7. George Clinton Densmore Odell, *Annals of the New York Stage* (New York: Columbia Univ. Press, 1928), 3: 146, 149, 249, 303, 380.

8. Tocqueville, 2: 85.

9. Margaret G. Watson, *Silver Theatre: Amusements of the Mining Frontier in Early Nevada 1850–1864* (Glendale, Calif.: Arthur H. Clark Co., 1964), p. 60.

10. Edmond McAdoo Gagey, *The San Francisco Stage, a History* (New York: Columbia Univ. Press, 1950), pp. 44–45.

11. Margaret Gardner Mayorga, *A Short History of the American Drama, Commentaries on Plays Prior to 1920* (New York: Dodd, Méad, 1944), p. 63; Willard, p. 75.

12. Iline Fife, "The Theatre During the Confederacy" (Ph.D. diss. Louisiana State University, 1949), p. 23.

13. Published by D. Longworth, at the Dramatic Repository, Shakespeare-Gallery, December 1812 and reprinted in *The Magazine of History* (Tarrytown, New York, 1931), vol. 43, no. 2, pp. 71–73. Additional verses in Dunlap's *Diary* (New York: New-York Historical Society, 1930), entry for 23 November 1812 in 2: 453 and for 20 February 1813, in 2: 467–68.

14. John Tasker Howard and George Kent Bellows, *A Short History of Music in America* (New York: Thomas Y. Crowell, 1959), p. 87.

15. The play is in Montrose Jonas Moses, ed., *Representative Plays by American Dramatists*, vol. 1, *1765–1819* (1918; rpt. New York: B. Blom, 1964), quotation p. 628.

16. Odell, 3: 322.

17. *The Diary of Philip Hone 1828–1851*, ed. Allan Nevins (New York: Dodd, Mead & Co., 1936), p. 837.

18. Micah Hawkins, *The Saw-Mill: Or a Yankee Trick. A Comic Opera*

in Two Acts . . . (1824; rpt. by W. Abbatt, Tarrytown, N.Y., 1927 in *The Magazine of History*, Extra number 127, vol. 32, no. 3), pp. 159–210.

19. Julian Mates, *The American Musical Stage before 1800* (New Brunswick, N.J.: Rutgers Univ. Press, 1962), p. 137.

20. Bertrand Evans, *Gothic Drama from Walpole to Shelley*, Univ. of California Publications in English, vol. 18 (Berkeley and Los Angeles, 1947), p. 163.

21. Maurice Willson Disher, *Melodrama: Plots that Thrilled* (New York: Macmillan, 1954), p. xiii.

22. Nicoll, *A History of English Drama, 1660–1900*, vol. 4, *Early Nineteenth-Century Drama, 1800–1850* (Cambridge: Cambridge Univ. Press, 1955), p. 87.

23. Ludlow, pp. 216–17.

24. David Grimsted, *Melodrama Unveiled; American Theatre and Culture, 1800–1850* (Chicago: Univ. of Chicago Press, 1968), Tables 7, 8, and 9, pp. 259, 260, and 261 respectively.

25. Grimsted, p. 237.

26. It was Alan Downer who pointed out, in a talk given at the American Theatre Festival, C. W. Post College, 1968, that, far from reforming, at the end the drunken Rip toasts the audience.

27. Hans Nathan, *Dan Emmett and the Rise of Early Negro Minstrelsy* (Norman: Univ. of Oklahoma Press, 1962), p. 113 ff.

28. Cited in Frank Costellow Davidson, "The Rise, Development, Decline and Influence of the American Minstrel Show" (Ph.D. diss., New York University, 1952), p. 74.

29. Cited in Blanche Muldrow, "The American Theatre as Seen by British Travellers 1790–1860" (Ph.D. diss., Univ. of Wisconsin, 1953), pp. 444–46.

30. Wilcomb E. Washburn, "The Great Autumnal Madness: Political Symbolism in Mid-Nineteenth-Century America," *Quarterly Journal of Speech* 49 (December 1963): 442.

31. *A History of the American Drama, from the Beginning to the Civil War*, 2d ed. (New York: F. S. Crofts & Co., 1943), pp. 267–68.

32. Montrose Jonas Moses, *The American Dramatist* (1925; rpt. New York: B. Blom, 1964), p. 92.

33. Theodore J. Shank, "Shakespeare and Nineteenth-Century Realism," *Theatre Survey* 4 (1963): 59.

34. David Krause, "The Theatre of Dion Boucicault," *The Dolmen Boucicault* (Dublin: The Dolmen Press, 1964), p. 13.

35. Daniel Frederick Havens, "The Development of a Native Tradition in Early American Social Comedy, 1787–1845" (Ph.D. diss., Univ. of Michigan, 1965), p. 8.

EDWARD JOHNSON AND THE

PURITAN TERRITORIAL IMPERATIVE

I

In some three centuries since its 1654 appearance, Edward Johnson's *Wonder-Working Providence* has suffered a not-always-benign neglect. Gouged for quotable nuggets of colonial cultural interest, and overshadowed by the multifarious literary productions of eminent New England divines and magistrates, Johnson's history has been, for want of an audience, largely ignored. It has been susceptible to occasional salvos for its anachronistic religious fervor or superannuated prosody, but only to muted praise for such intangibles as charm, energy, and vigor.[1] Happily, that state of affairs has been changing. Harold Jantz's progenitive appreciation for Johnson's "amazing sense of the truly epic," namely "the elevation of a set of local events into the universal under the span of a great unifying idea,"[2] opened the way for later studies by Ursula Brumm, Sacvan Bercovitch, and Edward Gallagher, whose essays have revealed a previously undisclosed "historiography rooted in biblical exegesis, embracing all of history, and fundamentally derived from the principles of typological interpretation."[3]

Still, aesthetic problems remain. Into that world of biblical metaphor Johnson intrudes racoons, locksmiths and brewers, and bushwacking, in a mimetic mode supposedly inferior to that of so erudite a divine as John Cotton, who in his argument with Roger Williams called the New England churches an enclosed garden in the wilderness, bounded by a protective hedge and threatened by heretical weeds that might choke the good herbs, should they overspread the garden.[4] Cotton's is a figure in the allegorical tradition of the enclosed garden, which is pervasive in seventeenth-century English literature. And while Edward Johnson, too, often invokes biblical figures spiritualized allegorically, his brewers, locksmiths, lead mines, and vast orchard acreage remain critically unaccounted-for. It is as if Matthew Brady had entered the world of the *Faerie Queene*, but only to be ignored. To read the growing number of Johnson's literary exegetes alongside the colonial cultural historians who have had recourse to the *Wonder-Working Providence*, one might think there existed two histories. One emerges as mythical and typologically cogent, and is represented in biblical symbols asserting New England's epic destiny. The other appears to chronicle the day-to-day progress of colonial life in a setting predominantly agricultural but technologically exploitable for its natural resources, having become congenially habitable through remarkable human industriousness and God's blessing.

But these two worlds, the mythic and the mundane, are conjoint in the *Wonder-Working Providence*, despite readers' polarization of them. And we distort the work until we recognize how and why Johnson binds up the Army of Christ with the Massachusetts Bay militia, and the textile mill with the forthcoming millennium. Indeed, Johnson's salient achievement was to fuse a bifocal world of earth and spirit in a literary weld of scriptural authority and seventeenth-century technics, all in a spirit of practicable utopianism. In retrospect it becomes clear that Johnson's singular literary achievement was to synthesize thematic possibilities broached but often not pursued in the writings of many of his Puritan contemporaries. Johnson's one major literary effort is, in fact, a splendid account of colonization exalted to cosmic status. It is invaluable because Johnson alone among the many Puritan colonial writers examined the material ramifications of the American New Jerusalem.

Johnson was, within the orthodox confines of millennial doctrine, a Puritan utopian. The term has been only tangentially applied to Puritan New England writings, largely because Calvinism blunted any Puritan notions of real human progress, and also because the Puritans themselves recoiled from the sin of pride by denying vehemently their intentions to make the New England commonwealth appositely a terrestrial urb and Augustinian City of God. (Late in the seventeenth century, of course, the ascendant tone of ministerial jeremiads lamenting New England's sins and corruptions would have made utopianism a bizarre, incongruous conception, except for the purpose of historical myth-making, which Sacvan Bercovitch finds to be Cotton Mather's motive for the invocation.) No doubt Edward Johnson would himself have balked at the suggestion of a utopian strain in his *Wonder-Working Providence*. He would affirm his genre as pure history, whose hallmarks were ethics, usefulness, and artful poesy —a compound put to describe changing surfaces of a world whose order God has fixed eternally, but permeated with providential interventions that revealed His divine plan.

Central to this godly pattern was a Reformation moving toward its biblically prophesied conclusion when the antichrist would be destroyed once and for all to usher in Christ's millennium, one thousand years of peace—as Cotton Mather put it, the very state "for which the whole creation groaneth." [5] Still, just as Clio in the seventeenth century was a muse often invoked on behalf of historiography, so there existed a futuristic obverse of her in the utopian projections of the Renaissance.

We have More, Andrea, Bacon, and Campanella side by side with Raleigh, John Smith, and Edward Johnson. Of course the Renaissance utopian worlds do spring fully developed into literature without the untidy process of trial and error that an historian must set forth, even if his record is one of human progression toward a heaven on earth.

The connection between such Puritans as Johnson and the Renaissance utopians is no temporal happenstance. A number of writers have discussed or mentioned the conceptual relationship between America and utopian projections.[6] More specifically, the Puritans themselves reveal a consciousness of it. Cotton Mather, attempting to innervate Boston's social and spiritual idlers, read to an audience part of a sermon whose author recalled New England life as free of beggery, cursing, and drunkenness. Mather concludes, "Shall I tell you where that Utopia was? 'Twas NEW ENGLAND!"[7] Puritan poet Benjamin Tompson had also revealed a utopian motif in his prefatory verse to William Hubbard's *Narrative of the Troubles with the Indians* (1677). Praising Hubbard's brave rendering of the native American setting, Tompson says,

> To treat of this New World our Author's bold.
>
> . . . .
>
> Unheard of places, like some *New-Atlantis*,
> Before in fancy only, now Newlandis.[8]

Utopian references for the sake of tortured rhyme or moral leavening do not, of course, constitute philosophical aspirations, but they do suggest a Puritan subliminal linkage between their own New England and the imaginative world of the utopian projector.

The connection surfaces consciously in William Hubbard's scornful critique of a failed plantation projected as Massachusiack under the patent of Robert Gorges. "By this experiment," says Hubbard, "it appears how great a difference there is between the theoretical and practical part of an enterprise.

The Utopian fancy of any projector may easily in imagination frame a flourishing plantation in such a country as was New England; but to the actual accomplishing thereof there is required a good number of resolved people qualified with industry, prudence, and estate, to carry on such a design to perfection, much of which were wanting in the present design." [9] Not by coincidence does Hubbard laud the exemplary Puritan fathers for possessing the very qualities necessary to the actual utopian accomplishment.

Lewis Mumford reminds us that the post-platonic utopia of the first 1500 years after Christ is called "the Kingdom of Heaven" and is "distinctly a utopia of escape." [10] But prefacing his discussions of Renaissance utopian writers, Mumford defines another sort of utopia, that of reconstruction. It is one which seeks to change—to reconstruct—the external world, even as it reforms the world of the spirit. This is a utopia that leads outward into the world to reconstitute it in a way better suited to the aspirations and the nature of man. Importantly, this utopia of reconstruction embraces both the mental *and* the terrestrial worlds—it is the new heaven *and* the new earth. As Edward Johnson wrote, "Some suppose this onely to be mysticall, and not literall at all: assuredly the spirituall fight is chiefly to be attended, and the other not neglected, having a neer dependancy one upon the other." [11]

And requisite to this utopia of reconstruction is a sense of futurity, else all is pointless. As Cotton Mather remarked, "We have a *Line of Time*, in the *Revelation*, drawn from the Resurrection of our Lord, unto that Kingdom, wherein He will give Peace unto us." [12] In Edward Johnson's Puritan milieu, the utopia was millennial, for the apocalyptic strain in the *Wonder-Working Providence* was no aberration from Puritan thought.

Within the past forty years a number of important studies have proven how pervasive was the apocalyptic sensibility of the New Englanders. Perry Miller recalls the colonists as children of a medieval people transacting daily business within sight of "terrifying realistic scenes of the last judgment . . . sculptured on the fronts of their churches and cathedrals." These colonial progeny "cherished still the vision of a glorious consummation" despite disquieting implications of Copernican physics that eventually undermined the traditional notion of the final conflagration.[13] (Indeed, the great popularity of Michael Wigglesworth's *Day of Doom* [1662] suggests that the New England Puritans had the Day of Judgment carved personally on the entablatures of their own minds.) Certainly Edward Johnson was attuned to the imminent apocalypse, for his was the belief, shared by many of his fellow Puritans both in England and America, that the prophesy of books 20 and 21 of Revelation was about to be realized. It decreed God's suppression of evil on earth, the chaining up of Satan, and the onset of the millennium, the thousand years of peace during which Christ would come to live and reign among His chosen people before loosing Satan for the final battle of the righteous against ultra-demonic peoples of Gog and Magog, whose defeat would signal the very end of human history and, for the chosen remnant, eternal heavenly bliss.

In the first of his two important books on apocalyptic thought in its various historical permutations, Ernest Tuveson points out how attentive were the Protestant Reformers to apocalyptic passages throughout the Old and New Testaments. Especially absorbing was the book of Daniel, which prophesies the defeat of four beasts (earthly kingdoms) after which the Son of Man will lead God's armies to a glorious victory. The Gospels also enumerate the portents of the end. "When ye therefore shall see the abomination of desolation spoken of by Daniel the prophet," warns Christ, "then let them which be in Judea flee into the mountains" (Matt. 24:15–16). The Nazarene had just explained the "abomination of desolation" in a catalog of human contentions and geophysical upheavals that signalled the inauguration of the millennium. But while Christ's prophesy suggests the imminence of the heavenly kingdom, the suggestion is, as Tuveson points out, vague, lacking the calendric precision of a historical moment.[14] For the Christian exegete this eschatological astigmatism could be overcome only by attending to Revelation, which provides a definite sequence of events, a timetable legible upon conversion of its many symbols into sequential periods and events of human history.

Although in Christian history millennial conceptions had shifted doctrinally from a chiliastic, cornucopian satisfaction of human wants to an Augustinian allegory bereft of any specific historical reference points, it was Luther who revamped the doctrine in the mold in which Johnson knew it. In 1545, just fifty-four years before Edward Johnson's birth, Luther wrote a second preface to the Apocalypse in which he suggested that man's incumbent duty is to penetrate the enigmatic prophesies in scripture. To render the symbols of Revelation—the seven-headed, ten-horned beast, the seven vials, the grapes of wrath, whore of Babylon, etc.—into historical events and periods, Luther devised the method that became the model for subsequent exegetes of scriptural prophesy. He correlated historical events with their referential symbols from Revelation.

The one crucial departure of Johnson and the New England Puritan divines from Luther's scheme of history is their projection of the millennium into the future. Luther had felt it was past, having begun roughly when St. John wrote down his vision, but one and one-half centuries later Cotton Mather was to remark that close study rendered such position untenable.[15] Had the New England divines not followed the lead of the English philosopher-theologian Joseph Mede in projecting the new earth of the millennium into the future, then Edward Johnson's *Wonder-Working Providence* could not have been written as a future-bent utopia of reconstruction, for Johnson would have viewed the human future as

severely truncated, and the power of human agency in creating the utopian new earth virtually nullified.

Johnson took a literal stance on one key point of apocalyptic doctrine. Others—very notably Increase and Cotton
Mather—expressed deeply-felt uncertainty about the location
and quality of the new earth, but not Johnson, for whom the
lodestone of history and prophesy pointed unerringly to New
England.[16] "For your full satisfaction," says his Christian
herald to the Puritans about to board their troop ship, "know
this is the place where the Lord will create a new Heaven, and
a new Earth in, new Churches, and a new Common-wealth
together" (p. 3). For Johnson New England was the site of
the New Jerusalem, literally. Just as medieval maps always
depicted the Holy Land as the center of the universe, so
Johnson conceived of the New Jerusalem as emanating
radially from New England in the millennium, "when not
onely the Assyrian, Babilonian, Persian, Grecian and Roman
Monarchies shall subject themselves unto him, but also all
other new upstart Kingdoms, Dukedoms, or what else can be
named, shall fall before him" (p. 11). Importantly, Johnson
did not believe that during the millennium Christ would
physically descend to earth, but rather that His spirit would
suffuse the universe. The thousand years of peace was to
him really a period of Christ's second advent. Those who
would believe otherwise, in his scornful view, "vainly imagine"
(p. 11). Johnson thus puts the creative burden of the millennial new earth squarely upon the Christian army of New
England colonists.

While Johnson's motives are apocalyptic, his justifications
for outreaching New England settlement are based largely on
the directives of Genesis, a source from which Puritans drew
exhaustive biblical authority for their emigration and land
appropriation in New England. In 1631 John Cotton wrote,
"Where there is a vacant place, there is liberty for the sonnes
of Adam or Noah to come and inhabite, though they neither

buy it, nor aske their [Indians'] leaves." [17] To John Eliot,
speaking of New England through the transparency of Old
Testament events, Noah's sons properly removed westward
because history had polluted "the Easterne world, the cursed
habitation of Cain and his posterity, where the floud-growing
sins did first spring up." [18] In retrospect Michael Wigglesworth, too, viewed the settlement of New England as an
exchange of turbulent history for spatial refuge:

> Here was the hiding place, which thou,
>   Jehovah, didst provide
> For thy redeemed ones, and where
>   Thou didst thy jewels hide
> In perlous times, and saddest dayes
>   Of sack-cloth and of blood,
> When th'overflowing scourge did pass
>   Through Europe, like a flood.[19]

Like all Puritan writers except the ever-dissenting Roger
Williams, Winthrop saw God's providential hand in the Indian
small pox deaths: "so the Lord hathe cleared our title to
what we possess. . . . so as God hathe cleared our title to
this place." [20]

Repeatedly Puritans discovered their New World deed
in Genesis. John White wrote, "Colonies have their warrent
from Gods direction and command, who, as soon as men
were, set their taske, to replenish the earth, and to subdue it,
Gen. 1.28." White asserts God's commandment as binding
throughout historical time as long as "the earth yields empty
places to be replenished," and he suggests that the prospective
colonists would in fact be neglectful, disobedient, and spiteful
of God *not* to emigrate.[21]

We find echoes of Genesis throughout Puritan colonial
literature. In his poem, "Uppon the first sight of New-England
June 29, 1638," Thomas Tillam wrote,

> Methinks I heare the Lambe of God thus speak
> Come my deare little flocke, who for my sake

> Have lefte your Country, dearest friends, and goods
> And hazarded your lives o'th raginge floods
> *Posses this Country* . . . . [italics mine] [22]

It was the possession of a hostile environment which Michael
Wigglesworth emphasized in a stanza whose speaker is awed
that a gracious God gave man dominion over fearsome lesser
creatures in the New England wilderness:

> The Lord had made (such was his grace)
>   For us a Covenant
> Both with the men, and with the beasts,
>   That in this desert haunt:
> So that through places wilde and waste
>   A single man, disarm'd
> Might journey many hundred miles,
>   And not at all be harm'd.
>
> Amidst the solitary woods
>   Poor travellers might sleep
> As free from danger as at home,
>   Though no man watch did keep.[23]

Further, Richard Steere in his poem about aesthetic attitudes
invokes both Genesis and the medieval idea of the hierarchical
Great Chain of Being. His man of the golden mean is "One,
who can as he list Compel the World/ To be his Servant."
"This man," says Steere, "owns God his Master, makes the
World his Slave." [24]

The proper extension of man's dominion on earth was, from
the Puritan perspective, the enlargement of Christ's kingdom
pointing toward the millennium. The psalmist asks, incredulous, "What is man, that thou art mindful of him?" then sings
exultantly of the excellence of the Lord's name in an earth
wherein man has "dominion over all the works of [God's]
hands" and "all *things* under his feet: all sheep and oxen, and
the beasts of the field, the fowl of the air, and the fish of the
sea, and whatsoever passeth through the paths of the seas"

(Psalm 8). Puritan inclusion of the Indians in the realm of their godly stewardship led John Cotton to remind the embarking colonists to "offend not the poore natives," but make them "partakers of your precious faith even as you partake in their land." [25] That philanthropic tone did not long endure in Puritan-Indian affairs, but from the outset of colonization Puritan dominion in the New World space is twofold: God makes room there for His chosen people, but the saints are themselves responsible for an enlargement of Christ's kingdom. One of Cotton Mather's wonders of the Invisible World was that God cast out the heathen (via a smallpox epidemic) to make room for his true Vine. Even after the horrible decimation of the English settlers in King Philip's War (1675–1677), William Hubbard could yet suggest that an important godly motive for the war was routing the Indians from "many *rich and Fertile places. . . .* whereby it may be gathered as we hope, that God is making way to settle a better people in their rooms, and in their stead." [26]

But the Puritan must actively expand Christ's kingdom. A contributor to the Eliot Tracts said of subsequent Puritan missionary work, "*Hereby the Kingdom of Christ is enlarged,* and the promise made unto him in the Covenant between him and his Father accomplished, his *Dominion shall be from Sea to Sea,* and from the floud unto the Worlds end, and therefore his designe is upon all the kingdoms of the Earth, that he may take possession of them." [27] In its proper perspective, man took dominion in order that Christ's dominion could be assured. The Lord created the earth "not in vain," but "to be inhabited" (Isaiah 45:18).

Before setting sail for New England the Puritans had anticipated the obvious objection that the land in their patent was not *vacuum domocilium,* but long in the possession of the Indians who were, as John Cotton put it, "Proprietaries of the places which [the Puritans will come to] inhabit." [28] It was John Winthrop who most comprehensively answered the demurral, invoking his favorite distinction between carnal naturalism and cultivated civility:

> That which lies comon & hath never been replenished or subdued is free to any that will possesse and improve it, for god hath given the sonnes of men a double right to the earth, there is a naturall right & a Civill right the first right was naturall when men held the earth in common every man soweing, and feeding where he pleased: and then as men and the cattle increased they appropriated certaine parcells of ground by enclosing, and peculiar manurance, and this in tyme gave them a Civill right. . . . And for the Natives in New England they inclose noe land neither have any settled habitation nor any tame cattle to improve the land by, & soe have noe other but a naturall right to those countries Soe as if wee leave them sufficient for their use wee may lawfully take the rest.[29]

Edward Johnson assents to Winthrop's distinction when, in the *Wonder-Working Providence*, he writes that the Indians need no provisioner in their camps "because they are continually at home" (p. 114) and "follow no kind of labour but hunting, fishing and fowling," with the result that they are "destitute of many necessaries, both in meat, drink, apparell and houses" (p. 225). Others reinforce Winthrop's position. An anonymous essayist remarked that "Improvement of all his sayd grownd . . . is one of the principall clauses of that grand Charter made by the greate Lord of the wholl earth and King of Nations unto Adam: Replenish the earth and subdue it."[30] John Eliot had similarly remarked that "the whole bent of mens mindes, in such Exigents [of dispersal] are to build, plant, fixe, and settle themselves in the places of their desire."[31] And though Eliot was speaking ostensibly of the dispersion and subsequent resettling of the Israelites after Nimrod's rebellion, he uses the biblical events as a metaphor for the New England planters fleeing England's own sectarian Babel.

Puritan efforts to legitimate their claim to New World lands by promising to subdue and improve it reveals itself in other ways as well. An *Abstract* of the early New England laws says that the basis of land assignment was "partly by the number of beasts, by the which a man is fit to occupy the land assigned to him, and subdue it." [32] Moreover, in the *Winthrop Papers* enough tenant-landlord squabbles have surfaced for us to understand that such improvement projects as fence mending and building, tree pruning, and repair to thatch and clapboard were contracted-for (as they were in the English counties), quite apart from the agreed-upon rent money. These obligations for improvement give special meaning to John Cotton's advice to the emigrants to "strive to attain the favor of your landlord [God], and be obedient to him" since he has provided shelter in a "foreine land." Again, Winthrop: "we deny that the Indians heere can have any title to more lands then they can improve . . . God gave the earth to be subdued, ergo a man can have no more than he can subdue." [33]

Statements like these are multiplied in Puritan writings, and in part reflect man's very oldest aspiration to conquer nature, in this instance by transposing domestic animals and agricultural methods to a wilderness. But the issue is more complex here. Vitally important in Winthrop's and his colleagues' logic is the position that improvement of the natural landscape constitutes civil right to it (and is prerequisite to a theological right). In other words, man evinces his dominion (and correlatively his stewardship over God's created world) by making a visible impress upon the natural world. He legitimates his claim to America by improving it manifestly. If we recognize in Puritanism an expression of the humanistic goals of a reconstruction both of man's spirit and of the world under the theological rubric primarily of Revelation ("a new heaven and a new earth") and of Isaiah ("shall a nation be born at once? for as soon as Zion travailed, she brought forth her children" [66:8]), then it is crucial that at the outset of colonization the Puritans would base their land claim upon an ability to make, literally, a mark upon America in the name of terrestrial improvement. Their theoretical justifications for claiming American land indicate that the Massachusetts Bay planters came not only to plant a spiritual garden of churches in the wilderness but that they sailed with a heavy duty incumbent upon them, namely an obligation to alter as much of the wilderness as could earn them their right to live there.

Because they had interpreted scripture so as to invalidate "natural" land rights in favor of "civil" ones in the name of earthly improvement and subjugation, the fear of terrestrial philandering weighed heavily upon the Puritan conscience. Failure to make a civilizing impress upon the land they claimed could invalidate their self-defined, biblically interpreted, rights to those lands. There was the danger, in short, that the Puritans might defeat themselves in the trap of their own logic. Thus they worried about land greed long before Cotton Mather uttered plaintive soul-searchings in the *Magnalia* about over-extension into the wilderness, and even before Edward Johnson inquired whether settlement beyond the sounds of ministerial trumpetings was fostering rural barbarism. In the early 1640s Nathaniel Ward had complained about "the lavish liberality of the [General] Court in giving away the Countrye." [34] Ward's sentiment was echoed by an essayist who deplored the "unwarantable greate extent of Townes . . . beyonde all hope of Subdoeing, or any Improvement." [35] Indian-war historian William Hubbard was to impute the firing of Medfield during King Philip's War to the folly of such overreaching. "The Inhabitants being every where apt to engross more Land into their hands than they were able to subdue," writes Hubbard, it was "as if they were seated in the midst of a heap of Bushes." [36] Edward Johnson, too, complains that the colonists' over-reach for meadow land "hath caused many towns to grasp more into their hands then they could afterward possibly hold" (p. 197). It is this Puritan undercurrent of anxiety about land greed that probably moved

Johnson to describe the various New England towns in aerial configurations. When he describes the fleur-de-lis, the human silhouette, the heart, and winged serpent, Johnson is acting less the whimsical cartographer than the vindicator of Puritan settlement. The familiar shapes indicate human definition of amorphous space, and in definition lies the making of the new earth.

Reading Johnson and others we come to realize that, geophysically, an American Lotus land would be anathema to their imperative to reform the environment, since an earthly paradise invites no reconstruction whatever. Mitigated toil in a more fertile river valley such as the Connecticut or Hudson is one thing, but Eden quite another. The Massachusetts marshlands are far better suited conceptually to the improvement or subjugation of the earth than is the Virginian Eden of the promotional tract. (In this regard the cessation of such effulgent accounts of New England as those of Francis Higginson and William Wood probably was due as much to the Puritan commitment to "improve" and "subdue" as it was to the grudging soil and abusive winters.) The Puritan reiteration of their commissioning to build a new earth in part by manifestly improving the New World may explain why such writers as Edward Johnson, Winthrop, and William Hubbard could, with certain qualifications, accept approvingly the geographic dispersal in the Northeastern part of the continent in a way they could not accept the departure of New Englanders for the Caribbean Islands, for Virginia, or even for that "full-fed land," England itself. In contrast to the rusticity of the Bay, England must have seemed in self-edited memory relatively paradisal. Something more than social desertion seems at issue in these cases. For the West Indies, the South, and the comforts of England were the fantasy of an escape to Eden in which improvement was inconceivable. If, as the historical geographer Yi-Fu Tuan remarks, the desert has been traditionally in the Western imagination a place inviting transformation for human use, then the Puritans' "desart wilderness," that ostensible tautology, may in fact have special meaning as the unsown place that compels man to take dominion by reconstituting it in a way that would be unthinkable in an earthly paradise.[37] Edward Johnson said himself that God deliberately imposed the onus of hardship, "knowing that had you met with a Rich Land filled with all plenty, your heart would have beene taken off this worke, which he must have done" (pp. 119–20).

II

The Bible offered the Puritans doctrines imparting cosmic meaning to their colonizing efforts; but representation of the endeavor in literature was another matter. Doctrinally, the directives of Genesis and the promises of Isaiah and Revelation enabled New Englanders to correlate the exigencies of colonial life with the theological imperatives of the spirit. Scripture thus made possible the connection between woodland hacking and hewing in Massachusetts and the purely spiritual (or, as Edward Johnson terms it, "mysticall") life of New England Puritanism. Difficult problems, however, remained for a writer attempting to render both of these areas of the Puritan colonial experience in language not confined to biblical metaphor.

Specifically, before the New England forest could be portrayed as the site of the New Earth, it was necessary that this forest (and swamp, and rock rubble, and even meadowland) first be invested with the values of the biblical wilderness. For just as the *Arbella* group arrived with *a priori* notions about land appropriation and forthcoming apocalyptic events, so had they firm preconceptions about the meaning of wilderness. Before they could write realistically—meaning, for the Puritans, theologically—about the unfamiliar topography at the sight of which Anne Bradstreet admitted her heart "rose," the Puritan writers had first to acknowledge the convergence of the palpable wilds of New England with the biblical wilderness of the Puritan mind's eye. In short, the spiritual wilderness had to find its objective correlative in the geography of New England. Until it did—that is, as long as Puritans thought of New England's wilds only as a *parallel* to the wilderness of the Bible—then Puritan writers would consistently invoke language of the Bible to render the New England experience within the confines of scriptural metaphor. (Moreover, when the early Puritans ventured into landscape description, as did Bradstreet, they were apt to revert to the bucolic England of memory, and in that way avoid the mimetic challenge—or perhaps onus—of reporting their optical views of the new setting.) But of course the wilds of New England were finally ineluctable to the Puritans, although evidence from their writings suggests that in literature the convergence of the actual and the spiritual wilderness took nearly twenty years.

Any concordance of colonial New England writings would show the words "wilderness," "desert," or even "waste" far surpassing in frequency the use of such less connotatively burdened terms as "land" or "ground," or the eulogistic "garden" or its Persian etymological equivalent, "paradise." Roderick Nash has shown that the colonists arrived in America with certain negative predispositions toward the American landscape, which they saw not only through the Bible, but through the lens of Anglo-Saxon myth and European history which abound with a dreadful menagerie of man-beasts supposed to inhabit gloomy uncivilized places.[38] Further, the Bible is replete with stories and themes based upon the precariousness of human life in a hostile natural environment. George Williams points out that "for the indigenous Canaanites the desert was peopled with dragons, demons, and monsters of the night."[39] In the Old Testament the wilderness geophysically is unarable land whose rainfall is insufficient to support crops and thus human life, in which sense it has far more to do with inadequate life support than with impenetrable verdure. But even land sown could not *per se* eradicate the wilderness, since it was not fixed geophysically, but shifted according to weather variation, thus lending itself to scriptural themes of Israel's moral advance or relapse. Expectedly, the Puritans' strong self-identification with the ancient Israelites led them to interpret agrarian bounty, scant harvest, and weather variance as God's manipulation of wilderness conditions so as to indicate His attitude toward the New English Israel.

Though fraught with negative connotations, "wilderness" is complicated by the cluster of biblically derived positive values as well, since it pertains not only to death, chaos, and punishment, but also to contemplation, insight, self-testing, sanctuary, and the promise of human fulfillment. These themes, coupled with the others, make it an ambiguous and tension-laden term in New England Puritan writings. Williams' excellent study, for which Peter Carroll has provided documentation from New England Puritan writings, delineates these varied meanings.[40] The wilderness is, first, "a place of redemptive, covenantal bliss" and a "place of testing and tutelage."[41] Erotic marriage figures such as those in Canticles ("Who *is* this that cometh up from the wilderness, leaning upon her beloved" [8:5]) evoke the covenantal bond. But conjointly there exists the theme of Israel tested in that wilderness ("And thou shalt remember all the way which the Lord thy God led thee these forty years in the wilderness, to humble thee, *and* to prove thee, to know what *was* in thine heart, whether thou wouldst keep his commandments, or no" [Deut. 8:2]).

Correlatively in the *Wonder-Working Providence* Edward Johnson represents Christ's herald as assuring the Puritan colonists that just as the Lord found the Jacobites "in the waste howling wilderness" and protectively cared for them

170   CECELIA TICHI

(Deut. 32:9), so "Assuredly (although it may now seeme
strange) you shall be fed in this Wildernesse, whither you are
to goe, with the flower of Wheate, and Wine shall be plenti-
full among you" (p. 4). Johnson's entire commissioning of the
New English Israel (Christ's army), which comprises the first
six chapters of his history, is a moral Baedeker for those yet
untried. His instructions about selecting magistrates, gathering
churches, avoiding temptations of toleration, abjuring land
greed, etc. are all a *vademecum* for those about to be tested
in the "desart wildernesse" according to those criteria.

   In addition to being a scene of spiritual testing, the biblical
wilderness is also a haven and place of purgation or of consecration. The seer of Revelation describes the exile of "the
woman fled into the wilderness, where she hath a place prepared of God, that they should feed her there a thousand two
hundred *and* threescore days" (Rev. 12:6). Moreover, the
Prophet Elijah retreated to the wilderness and, at God's command, annointed a King in the desert (1 Kings 19), which is
thus the place of consecration. In addition, after his baptism
in the Jordan, Christ was tempted by Satan in the wilderness,
and John the Baptist preaching in the desert embodies the
ascetic ideal of wilderness as a sanctuary and site of faith
strengthened and purified. Further, the Seer of Revelation
(1:9; 17:3) suggests that a wilderness retreat enables man to
see God more profoundly. Such ascetic wilderness values
appear contrary to paradisal ones, but since a wilderness
condition may be God's testing or even punishment, the conclusion that is implicit in that punitive period is an attainment
of paradise. The Lord promises to "make the wilderness a pool
of water, and the dry land springs of water" (Isaiah 41:18). In
this sense Israel endures temptations and suffers punishment
for its sins, but always with the promise of paradise to be
regained.

   To encounter in New England Puritan writings the terms
"wilderness" or "desert," or the contrary "garden," "paradise"

(or such biblical extensions as vine or vineyard), is, then, to
apprehend the great extent to which these terms refer more to
spiritual states than to geophysical properties. In his exposition
of the sixteenth chapter of Revelation John Cotton writes that

> All the world is a wildernesse, or at least a wilde field; onely,
> the Church is Gods garden or orchard, in these three respects,
> First, as the garden of Paradise was the habitation of Adam in
> the estate of innocense, so is the Church of all those who are
> renewed into innocency.
> Secondly, as in the garden were all manner of pleasant and
> wholesome hearbs and trees growing, so in the Church are all
> manner of usefull and savoury spirits.
> Thirdly, as a man walketh in his garden to refresh himselfe;
> so doth Christ walke in his Church, yea calleth his friends
> thither to walke with him.[42]

At certain points in the *Wonder-Working Providence* Edward Johnson too draws upon these images, which derive
immediately from scripture. "Christ's vineyard" and "this
Vineyard of the Lord" hearken to the Gospels and not to New
England viniculture. Perhaps one of the most thoroughly
spiritualized wilderness referents from scripture occurs in
this passage from the Eliot Tracts:

> This in Generall wee may say, that in the Wilernesse are
> waters broken out, and streames in the Desert, the parched
> ground is become a Poole, and the thirsty Land-springs of water
> in the Habitation of Dragons, where each lay, there is grasse
> with Reeds and Rushes, the Lord hath powred water upon him
> that is thirstie, and flouds upon the dry ground.[43]

In wholly symbolic language from Isaiah the writer is speaking about successful Puritan missionary efforts among the
Indians. The reader must himself draw the connections between the topic and the language in which it is conveyed.
The particular New England wilderness and its red-skinned
populace is entirely subsumed in the language of the Bible,

which imparts to it cosmic significance for the colonial exegete, whether writer or reader.

Wilderness in the literature of seventeenth-century New England remains to this day elusive and protean not only because the word includes the complex of biblical definitions and values, but because in Puritan usage it constantly shifts between literal and abstract levels of reference and between pejorative and eulogistic connotations, sometimes in works of the same author, and often in a single piece of writing. Notwithstanding these problems of interpretation, it is evident that despite myriad usage, "wilderness" by the late 1640s embraced two worlds, the spiritual one of biblical history and prophesy, and the earthly one of New England's own topography. For the former, the New England wilderness was a spiritual world, not a landscape but an inscape. It was a metaphoric reality enlarged in value by its thematic apposition to scriptural meanings of wilderness, desert, and garden. As long as it remained so, then that metaphoric reality could be quite separate from the palpable landscape in which civil issues emerged from the exigencies of pioneer life. When the Connecticut Puritan minister Joseph Morgan writes repeatedly of a "Wilderness of Pleasures," we are certain of allegory that has nothing to do with New England.[44] The two realms —of scriptural inscape and civil landscape—are, in fact, quite distinguishable, connected primarily by the Puritan conviction that a topographical impress of civilization must precede the diffusion of Christianity.

But Puritan writings before 1650 indicate that the palpable landscape was increasingly impinging upon the metaphoric wilderness of biblical expression. John Wilson's language demonstrates this:

> But me thinkes now that is with the Indians as it was with our New-English ground when we first came over, there was scarce any man that could beleeve that English graine would grow, or that the plow could doe any good in this woody and rocky

soile. And thus they continued in this supine unbeliefe for some
years, till experience taught them otherwise . . . so wee have
thought of our Indian people, and therefore have been discour-
aged to put plow to such dry and rock ground but . . . it may
be they are better soile for the Gospel than wee can think. . . .
'Tis no small matter that such dry barren and long-accursed
ground should yield such kind of increase in so small a time.[45]

Here the civil, godly commitment to land improvement by
planting is analogous to spiritual reform of the Indians who
are a part of the landscape. But the language of this statement
indicates a convergence of civil and spiritual wilderness. When
John Wilson tramped through fallen leaves in the November
woods to catechize the Indians, offering them goodwill tokens
of tobacco and apples, he was enacting the spiritual wilderness work. But unlike his colleague Henry Whitfield, Wilson
chose to express the import of that work, not in the readily-
available language of the Bible with its preconditioned reader
responses, but in the terms of New England's own agriculture.

Lacking the poetry of Scripture, Wilson's rhetoric sounds
pedestrian. But aesthetics aside, his statement indicates an
emergent intellectual reciprocity between a biblical wilderness and a New England forest. That they should merge was
inevitable because, as William Hubbard said, ancient Israel
had but to pass through the wilderness, and not to plant it as
did Puritans in New England.[46] Thus twenty years after the
Winthrop "planting" we see inscape and landscape drawn
close together in such of Edward Johnson's phrases as "western wast," "wilderness of rocks," and "wild-woody wilderness." The geographical locus of the West, the rockiness of
land irrespective of scriptural stones of Jacob or Samuel, the
semantic and alliterative link between virgin forest and scriptural wilderness—all these work toward connection of the
palpable and spiritual. They reveal the great extent to which
American topographical and geophysical properties were making incursions upon the *a priori* scriptural wilderness the

Puritans thought themselves in before ever they arrived on
New World shores.

This continuous impinging of the worlds of soil and spirit
made Puritan literature ripe for the literary imagination that
might truly synthesize the two in language drawn from both
realms, and informed with a vision at once earthly and
heavenly. As it came about, Edward Johnson's was that
imagination.

III

More of an activist than an ideologue, Johnson prefers to
prove the creation of the new earth less in metaphysics than
in material fact. Doctrinally Johnson's New Jerusalem derives from the ministers, whose imaginations gave it life in
figures congenial to their own habits of mind, for instance in
metaphors of arrows lancing sin-hardened hearts. But in
Johnson we see the doctrine vivified in the mind of an activist-
colonizer prone to figures denoting huge resources of available power. Apart from reportage, he depends upon the
central military metaphor to be both typologically true and
polemically plausible in his story. Moreover, by emphasizing
the importance of human labor in expediting the Christian
millennium, Johnson can find in the dreariest of colonial toil
certain apocalyptic value, and reserve for man an active role
in bringing about the prophesied new earth. His conviction
that the millennial epoch would begin in New England and
that Christ would be present in spirit only tended to reinforce
his belief in the franchised power of the saints.

For the clear thrust of these attitudes is to make the saints
responsible for attaining of the millennial state. In the nice
balance of social Christian spirit among a people joined to the
New England earth, Johnson rivets attention to the human
role in millennial preparation. He adduces apocalyptic values
from colonizing work and thus removes from the millennium

such hints of human passivity as are implicit in other Puritans'
visions of Christ and angels suddenly descending to earth.
Their Paradise would be regained by godly fiat, but the cost
would be the nullification of human value in the active hus-
bandry and gardening and technics so vital in Johnson's
scheme of things. The actual work of colonization would, in
short, be negligible. Thus it is not at all surprising that Johnson should reject the notion of a millennium inaugurated by
God in a context of human passivity. On the contrary, he
asserts human labor as necessary to the realization of the
American New Jerusalem.

A look at that seemingly bumptious title—*The Wonder-
Working Providence of Sions Savior in New England*—immediately reveals Sion's (Zion's) savior as Christ who, having
redeemed man by his death, works awesome wonders by
guiding and directing Puritan New England, which is the true
Zion, the New English Israel. But just as "providence" indicates godly direction, so it also implies foresight or preparation for the future, in which sense it is vitally important in
Johnson's scheme of history.

Semantically "Working" adumbrates two meanings crucial
to Johnson's story of a New World transformed. First, God's
"working" providence is operational; it brings about the awesome wonders. Johnson had written in *Good News from
New England* of "the great *Jehova's working word* [my
italics] effecting wondrously/ This earths vast globe, those
parts unknown." [47] But the title of his history further con-
veys the notion of work as labor, which is the key to his
story of a wilderness transformed, and to his idea of the appropriate relationship of Puritan to Christ in New England.

In his opening chapters when Christ's army is commissioned and empowered, Johnson cautions that continuous
energy can flow only from Christ. But in a leaden pun the
herald warns, "So soone as you shall seeke to ingrosse the
Lords wast into your hands, he will ease you of your burden

by making stay of any further resort unto you, and then be
sure you shall have wast Land enough." This punster gives
the full meaning of "Working" in Johnson's title and text:
God's is the power which, imparted to the Puritan troops,
will be wondrously operational *through man's labor*. "All
men that expect the day, must attend the means."

The virtue of Johnson's work ethic lies, then, in its millennial expedience. The New Earth is to be man-made. Possibilities of this theme had engaged him even in *Good News*,
in which Indians are naked men "whom labour did not tame,"
and the colonists initially in straits "till labour blesse the earths
encrease . . . the land being sowne with man and beast." We
see "the Husband-man rejoycing," and a panoply of grain
crops brought to exportive surplus by the "Plough-man." The
edenic oysters are not relished for succulence (nor even for
comparison to the then-famous oyster beds of Johnson's native Kent), but for conversion of their shells for lime "to lay
fast stone and brick." Prefacing a paean to twenty Puritan
ministers in that poem, Johnson wrote:

> What creature man that is apt to take
>   His praise, who work and workman both did make
> In telling of these Worthies work then I
>   Own none but God, and yet his meanes I eye.

In the *Wonder-Working Providence* Johnson further developed his theme of spiritual and manual labor spent on behalf of the New Earth effort. He never once relents by yearning for the New Earth by godly fiat. Even at the conclusion
of the *Wonder-Working Providence* his gauntlet is down:
"You that long so much for it, come forth and fight; who can
expect a victory without a battel?"

Not that Johnson alone among Puritan writers gave witness
to the visible transformation of the landscape through hard
work. Benjamin Lynde extols the beauties of a Boston in-
trinsically satisfying as a city-scape:

Enrang'd street under street, she forms below
A beauteous crescent, or Heaven's painted Bow
Of various hewes; at either end a fort
Defends her boosome and adorns her port.
From her rich centre structures, saches bright
Reflect the blushes of Aurora's light,
And golden spires by turnes waved high in air
Seem planets, Venus, or the Morning Star. (lines 64–70) [48]

He goes on to sing the esthetic pleasures of pier and ware-
house full of merchandise. As his fellow Puritan versifier Grindall Rawson put it, "Citizens of the New Jerusalem . . .
Rightly improve their towne." [49]

Other Puritan writers use the obvious transformation of
the New England landscape as a caveat against worldliness
or ingratitude to God. William Bradford is one:

> O Boston, though thou art now grown
> To be a great and wealthy town,
> Yet I have seen thee a void place,
> Shrubs and bushes covering thy face;
> And house then in thee none were there
> Nor such as gold and silk did weare;
> No drunkenness were then in thee,
> Nor such excess as now we see.

Bradford warns Bostonians—or those in a two-urbane "Boston condition"—to recall their humbler origins and the great
moral leadership of their founders. He warns them not to de-
file the land in materialistic trafficking: "The trade is all in
your own hand,/ Take heed ye doe not wrong the land." [50]
Like Bradford, John Higginson uses the visible metamorphos-
ing of wilderness into prosperous settlement to remind the
Puritan burghers that thanks go to God alone. "Many earthly
comforts," "small beginnings to great estates," "townes &
fields," "shops and ships"—all visible signs of civilization invite a resounding *No!* to the rhetorical question from Jere-

miah 2:32, "O generation see the word of the Lord, have I
been a wilderness to you?" [51]

Apart from his literal-mindedness, one major difference between Johnson and these others is that they portray the re-
formed new world landscape as a *fait accompli*, whether for
good or ill, depending upon their rhetorical purposes. But
theirs is a static view, a kind of "before" and "after" diptych.
Johnson, on the other hand, is vitally concerned to portray the
process of reconstruction, the dynamic movement through
which the new earth emerges—the Wonders Work*ing*. True,
at several points he hearkens to that "instant" nation of
Isaiah 66:8. But Johnson validates his Isaihan bravura with
accounts of the labor involved. Indeed, the *Wonder-Working
Providence* is very much a story of America earned through
the toil of settlers.

These emigrants forswear, in the incredulous view of their
English friends and acquaintances (as Johnson represents
them), both well-plenished tables and coin-filled coffers, as
well as beautifully built and richly appointed houses. Johnson
admits "the first beginning of this worke seemed very dolor-
ous" (p. 38). Though scurvied, they begin in "steddy resolution . . . to plant the yet untilled Earth, having as yet no
other meanes to teare up the bushy lands, but their hands and
howes" (p. 53). Men unaccustomed to manual labor "fall to
tearing up the Roots and Bushes with their Howes." "Cutting
down of the Woods, they inclose Corne fields" (p. 56).
"Standing stoutly to their labours," they "teare up the Roots
and Bushes." And though forced to go barefooted at first,
there are none "so barbarously bent" that they do not gather
churches, even though "the toile of a new Plantation, being
like the labours of Hercules, [is] never at an end." Ever
strengthened by Christ, singing psalms and praising God, "in
these poore Wigwames," the colonists nonetheless are at times
grievously in a "lonesome condition" (pp. 83–84). But, in
Christian "love and unity," the settlers are "translating the

close, clouded woods into goodly cornfields" (p. 126). The high purpose coupled with endurance and, ultimately, triumph over nature's abrasions elevates the effort to epic status. Because an apocalyptic destiny draws these people into uncharted terrain, no reader is inclined to scoff at hyperbole when Johnson calls the effort Herculean. He truly renders it so in his narrative. New England may be a nation brought forth in a day, but Johnson evokes a strong sense of the horrendous human midwifery involved.

Many aspects of Johnson's chronicle of the process of reconstruction of the American landscape seem based upon English models. For instance the swamp trekking seems based upon similar efforts in England. The social and economic historian of seventeenth-century Kent, C. W. Chalklin, writes that "the principal means [of forest clearance] seem to have been the building of farmsteads in the forest, and the gradual clearance of the surrounding land." [52] One is well reminded that Johnson was born at the very turn of the sixteenth century, and was all of thirty years old when he sailed on the *Arbella*—just five years short of the average life expectancy in Kent. When we read his boasts about American trees felled and vast acreage planted in orchards, we are listening in large part to amplified echoes of contemporary English (and particularly Kentish) life. Throughout England in the sixteenth and early seventeenth centuries a rising population "led to the clearance of woods, the enclosure of moorland, and the drainage of marshes and fens on a scale unknown for at least two hundred years." [53] In a predominately agricultural economy, arability of land determines value, and potential for reclamation is a touchstone of worth. When William Hubbard wrote bitterly of the English blood spilled in the cause of Indian suppression in the Maine region, his complaint was based upon the worthlessness of the Maine land, "a barren and Rocky Country . . . being of little worth, unless it were for the Borders upon the Sea-coast and some spots and

Skirts of more desirable Land upon the banks of some Rivers." [54] An anonymous essayist proposed that each New England colonist allotted land for home and farm ought also to be burdened with an equal proportion of "Swampes and such Rubbish waest grounds . . . which harbor Wolves and such noyesome beasts and serpents," which the settler would be obliged to clear, in order that such ground "may be suppressed." [55] The attitude of the Lynn town fathers toward a marshland too vast to be reclaimed emerges in the language of their petition to the General Court for "some competent allowance unto so good a work as the erecting of a bridge" over "the Flatts and rottennesse of the Marsh." [56] Johnson, too, invokes such phrases as "western wast," "terrible Wildernesse," "Wilderness of Rocks," etc.—all of which enhance the triumph of his proclamation that "the constant penetrating farther into this Wilderness hath caused the wild and uncouth woods to be fil'd with frequented wayes, and the large rivers to be over-laid with Bridges passeable both for horse and foot" (p. 197). For Johnson the triumph is based upon New England's successful emulation of the dynamic landscape alteration which he had witnessed since his boyhood.

The making of the new earth is in Johnson largely a function of agriculture, not from a Hesiodic ideal, but from necessity. "After the flood," wrote Eliot, "Noah began to be an husbandman, as all men usually do in new plantations, whatever their occupations were formerly." [57] Throughout the *Wonder-Working Providence* Johnson has recourse to the enormity of the toil, but never does he exalt drudgery. He is pleased to say that after the initial settlement, "the Lord hath taught them to labour with more ease" and that "whereas at their first coming it was a rare matter for a man to have foure or five Acres of Corne, now many have four or five score" (p. 120). "Neer a thousand acres of land" are "planted for Orchards and Gardens, besides their fields are filled with garden fruit" (p. 175). Johnson has been criticized for his

statistical errors, but to know that in his native Kent a farm
of five to ten acres often supported an entire family, and that
orchards and gardens ran to less than one acre is to recognize
the propagandistic value of the new earth affirmed in statistics
bespeaking fantastic abundance realized through man's labor
with God's blessing.[58] Recurrently in Johnson we see environmental restructuring with an eye toward the amelioration of life in New England. For Winthrop the Indian land
claims were invalid because the natives had "no artes, cattle,
or other menes to subdue or improve any more of those lands
then they plant with Corne." Winthrop does not elaborate
upon Puritan "artes" or "menes," but Johnson's imagination is
rife with possibilities presaging America's technocracy. Specifically, Johnson's new earth is attainable not only through
tillage, but through human mechanization and invention.

There is a technological side to the Puritan imagination,
one not much observed, in large part because discussions of
Puritan tribalism have invited close attention to organic metaphors of community, but not to those figures suggesting the
uniform discipline and synchonized movement of machinery.
For instance, we recall Cotton Mather's "a vine here planted"
which God has "Caus[ed] to take deep Root, and fill the
land, so that it sent its boughs unto the Atlantic Sea Eastward,
and its Branches unto the Connecticut Westward, and the
Hills covered with the shadow thereof." [59] Though Edward
Johnson had access to the scriptural font of botanical images
(and used them somewhat), he much preferred to draw upon
the military figures of the Bible (2 Timothy 2:3), which were
also widespread in Puritan writings. Johnson's autobiographi-
cal affinity with soldiery makes his choice appear naive and
facile, even if such figures were intended to engender the
security of godly specialness of the Puritan heart, and provide
assurance that colonial soldiery of the spirit was every bit as
important as the Cromwellian sort.

But whether drafted, enlisted, or commissioned for Christ,

the army has military implications impossible of conveyance in organic figures of vines and trees. An army is disciplined and synchronized in movements. Its strength is concentrated, its power an exponential multiple of one individual's capability. Collectively it is a superhuman machine into which the individual submerges his personal identity for the greater glory of the whole. John Winthrop's often-cited warning aboard the *Arbella* that society must maintain its fixity of interlocking classes has been viewed as reflective of a medieval socioeconomic structure soon to disappear in entrepreneurial America; but it also suggests the Puritan conviction about the virtue of a disciplined social machine whose components assent to the common work goal. As John Eliot wrote, "Grounds and ends are secret things from the sight of other men . . . and therefore the best to prove unto men that our grounds and ends are Religious, is to let it appear to be so, by our religious waies and works." [60]

The particularly Christian themes in the *Wonder-Working Providence*, especially those of Christ's parental and the oft-evoked apocalyptic destiny of New England, prevent Johnson's soldiers from becoming automatons in a huge colonizing machine, though elsewhere in Puritan writings there emerges a desire for such machinery. Emmanuel Downing suggested that Indian captives be exchanged for black slaves, since, he says, "oure childrens children will hardly see this great Continent filled up with people," and thus "[I] doe not see how we can thrive untill wee gett into a stock of slaves sufficient to do all our business." [61] The heavy work of smelting iron created enough labor difficulties for the managers of the Lynn iron works to import a group of Scottish prisoners as slaves.[62] And even in John Eliot's account of Indian missionary work there is a great value placed upon the mobilization of efficient units engaged in transforming wilderness into civilization. For Edward Johnson the new earth construction, as well as the final battle against Gog and Magog demand, both spiritually and literally, a military preparedness, but on New England's side is the orderly, controlled, powerful social machine of an army, while the forces of antichrist are comprised of the human disorder, the dissipated strength, the mobocracy of a "whole rabble" (p. 195).

Apart from human mechanization, Johnson shows strong interest in the possibilities of invention, the other harbinger of the technocracy. John White had said it in 1629: the "shifting into empty lands, enforceth men to frugality, and quickeneth invention." [63] And John Eliot observes that Noah's age had no doubt mastered oenology, since "they had inventions of far greater consideration, and difficulty." [64] We recall, too, Edward Taylor's Preparatory Meditation 2.56 in which works of God "out vie both works of nature and of Art," but only after Taylor has listed an impressive array of ingenious mechanical devices. Edward Johnson enthusiastically partakes of this interest in mechanics, but as indices of sophisticated improvement in New England life. The "iron mill in constant use," the "fulling-mill" that enabled Rowley's people to be the "first that set upon making of Cloth in this Western World," the "saw-mills," "The Corn mill," the catalogue of artisans now freed from the plow to follow such technical crafts as smithing, tinkering, turning, pumpmaking—all this exploitation of technics is to Johnson a sign of human amelioration among the New England soldiers of Christ. The technics and disciplined social structure are the instruments of terrestrial reconstruction. They are the "artes" and the "menes" that Winthrop found wanting among the Indians. They have transformed thickets of suckling wolves and bears into "streets full of Girles and Boys sporting up and down" in a Boston whose "continuall inlargement presages some sumptuous City," even if the Royal Commissioners in 1666–67 sniffed at crooked streets "with little decency and no uniformity" and belittled the "wooden college" which Johnson cherished for its conversion of wilderness into parietal "bowl-

184   CECELIA TICHI

ing green" (p. 164).[65] Johnson's recourse to a variety of ma-
chines and crafts, and his boast that in New England a large
group of mechanics "follow their trades only," having "left
the husbandmen to follow the Plow and Cart" (p. 209), be-
speak a new earth in which machine and garden co-exist
amicably, conjoint with reconstructed (or, in Johnson's term,
purified) religious and political institutions. Johnson's new
earth may be scented acridly with the gunpowder of Christ's
artillery, but its godly engineering is just one function of the
dynamic conversion of amorphous new world space into the
utopian demesne of the American New Jerusalem.

CECELIA TICHI
BOSTON UNIVERSITY

Notes

1. See Helmut Richard Niebuhr, *The Kingdom of God in America*
(1935; rpt. Hamden, Connecticut: Shoe String Press, 1956), p. 47; Charles
L. Sanford, *The Quest for Paradise* (Urbana: Univ. of Illinois Press, 1961),
p. 83; Peter Gay, *A Loss of Mastery* (Berkeley: Univ. of Calif. Press, 1966),
p. 53; Perry Miller and Thomas H. Johnson, *The Puritans* (New York:
Harper & Row, 1963), pp. 1, 90; Moses Coit Tyler, *A History of American
Literature, 1607–1765* (New York: Collier, 1962), p. 143; Richard S. Dunn,
"Seventeenth-Century English Historians of America," in *Seventeenth-
Century America*, ed. James Morton Smith (Williamsburg, Va.: Univ. of
North Carolina Press, 1959), pp. 204–5; Michael Kraus, *The Writing of
American History* (Norman: Univ. of Oklahoma Press, 1953), pp. 27–28;
and Kenneth Ballard Murdock, *Literature and Theology in Colonial New
England* (1949; rpt. New York: Harper & Row, 1963), pp. 86–88. Johnson
is called "vigorous," "imaginative," and "enthusiastic," but also a "rustic
trumpet," "some minor player in the orchestra," "burdened by rhetorical
flights," "verbose," "turgid," "crude in thought and style," "not an artist
but a woodworker."

2. Harold Jantz, *The First Century of New England Verse* (1944; rpt.
New York: Russell and Russell, 1962), p. 23.

3. Sacvan Bercovitch, "The Historiography of Johnson's *Wonder-
Working Providence*," *Essex Institute Historical Collections*, 104, 2 (1968),
142; see also Ursula Brumm, "Edward Johnson's *Wonder-Working Providence* and the Puritan Conception of History," *Jahrbuch für Amerika
studiesn* 14 (1969): 140–51. Edward J. Gallagher, "An Overview of Edward

Johnson's *Wonder-Working Providence*," *Early American Literature* 3 (1971): 30–49, discusses the work "in relation to its contemporary purpose and cultural moment" (30).

4. John Cotton, *The Bloudy Tenant Washed* . . . (London, 1647), p. 151.

5. Cotton Mather, *Thoughts for a Day of Rain* . . . (Boston, 1712), p. 2.

6. See Alfred Leslie Rowse, *The Elizabethans and America* (New York: Harper, 1959), pp. 188–89; Arthur William Plumstead, *The Wall and the Garden: Selected Massachusetts Election Sermons 1670–1775* (Minneapolis: Univ. of Minnesota Press, 1968), p. 180; Daniel J. Boorstin, *The Americans; The Colonial Experience* (New York: Random House, 1958), pp. 29–31. Russel B. Nye, "Michel-Guillaume St. Jean De Crevecoeur: *Letters from an American Farmer,*" in *Landmarks of American Writing*, ed. Hennig Cohen (New York: Basic Books, 1969), pp. 32–33, hints that Edward Johnson is a Puritan utopian. Hawthorne's derision of Puritan utopianism indicates belief that his forebears saw themselves as utopians. See Nathaniel Hawthorne, *The Scarlet Letter* (1850), ed. Sculley Bradley, Richard Croom Beatty, and E. Hudson Long (New York: Norton, 1962), p. 3.

7. Cotton Mather, *Magnalia Christi Americana, Or; The Ecclesiastical History of New England*, ed. Rev. Thomas Robbins (Hartford, Conn.: S. Andrus and Son, 1855), 1: 103. Sacvan Bercovitch argues that Mather invokes the idea of a utopian New England past when in his imagination he re-writes the Puritan past as myth. See "Horologicals to Chronometricals," in *Literary Monographs*, vol. 3 (Madison, Milwaukee, and London: Univ. of Wisconsin Press, 1970), pp. 1–124.

8. Benjamin Tompson, "Upon the Elaborate Survey of New-Englands Passions," in William Hubbard, *The Present State of New England* . . . (London, Printed for The Parkhurst, 1677).

9. William Hubbard, *General History of New England from the Discovery to MDCLXXX* (Cambridge, Mass.: Hilliard & Metcalf, 1815), p. 87.

10. Lewis Mumford, *The Story of Utopias* (1922; rpt. New York: Viking, 1962), p. 57. This discussion is much indebted to Mumford's *Technics and Civilization* (1934; rpt. New York: Harcourt, Brace & World, 1963), and to his *The Myth of the Machine: Technics and Human Development* (New York: Harcourt, Brace & World, 1967) and *The Myth of the Machine: The Pentagon of Power* (New York: Harcourt Brace Jovanovich, 1970).

11. Edward Johnson, *The Wonder-Working Providence of Sions Saviour in New England and Good News from New England*, ed. Edward J. Gallagher (Delmar, N.Y.: Scholars' Facsimiles & Reprints, 1974), p. 232.

12. Cotton Mather, *Things to be Look'd For* . . . (Boston, 1691), p. 35.

13. Perry Miller, "The End of the World," in *Errand Into the Wilderness* (1956; rpt. New York: Harper, 1964), pp. 217–18. The Puritans' apocalyptic

sensibility has been well documented since the appearance of H. Richard Niebuhr's *Kingdom of God in America* (op. cit.), and Harold Jantz's remark on the "transcendental, apocalyptic, millennarian, utopian tendencies which were so strong in many of the leaders (Cotton, Hooker, Davenport, Chauncy, the younger Winthrop, etc.)" (op. cit., p. 25). See also Charles L. Sanford (op. cit.); Alan Simpson, *Puritanism in Old and New England* (Chicago: Univ. of Chicago Press, 1955), pp. 75–79; and LeRoy Edwin Froom, *The Prophetic Faith of our Fathers* . . . (Washington, D.C.: Review and Herald, 1946), 1: 1–207. For a discussion of popular millennial thought during the Middle Ages see Norman Rufus Colin Cohn, *The Pursuit of the Millennium* (1957; rpt. London: Temple Smith, 1970). Two important works on the subject are Ernest Lee Tuveson, *Millennium and Utopia* . . . (Berkeley and Los Angeles: Univ. of Calif. Press, 1949) and *Redeemer Nation: The Idea of America's Millennial Role* (Chicago: and Univ. of Chicago Press, 1968). Though Tuveson does not discuss in depth millennial strains in seventeenth-century Puritan New England, Sacvan Bercovitch confronts the implications of millennial thought in the Puritan jeremiads. See "Horologicals to Chronometricals" (op. cit.). Robin George Collingwood remarked that "any history written on Christian principles will be of necessity universal, providential, apocalyptic, and periodized." See his *The Idea of History* (Oxford: Clarendon Press, 1946), p. 46.

14. *Millennium and Utopia*, p. 9.

15. Cotton Mather, *Things to be Look'd For*, pp. 1–7.

16. Increase Mather's anti-chiliastic bias is evident in the "Preface," *Discourse Concerning Faith and Fervency of Prayer* . . . (Boston, 1710), but he remarks that in the millennium the world "will be restored to its paradise state" (p. 57). Cotton Mather, *Remarks upon the Changes of a Dying World* . . . (Boston, 1715), admits uncertainty about whether the earth will exist eternally or not, then oxymoronically asserts that the "Dissolution that comes at the *Conflagration* . . . will not be the Destroying of the Earth, so much as the refining of it" (p. 15). Robert Middlekauf, *The Mathers* (New York: Oxford Univ. Press, 1971), discusses Cotton Mather's gratification in "the grand smash of all things," followed by the New Jerusalem contained in the New Heavens (pp. 328–31). But he omits consideration of the *Theopolis Americana* (Boston, 1710), in which the new earth is especially American.

17. John Cotton, *Gods Promise to His Plantation* . . . (Boston, 1630), p. 4.

18. John Eliot, "The Learned Conjectures," in Thomas Thorowgood, *Jews in America* . . . (London, Printed by W. H. for T. Slater, 1650), 4.

19. Michael Wigglesworth, *God's Controversy with New-England*, in *Seventeenth-Century American Poetry*, ed. Harrison T. Meserole (Garden City, N.Y.: Doubleday, 1968), p. 45.

20. John Winthrop, *Winthrop Papers*, 2 (Boston: Massachusetts Historical Society, 1944), 3: 167, 172.

21. John White, *The Planters Plea*, in Peter Force, *Tracts and Other Papers* . . . (Washington, D.C., printed by P. Force, 1838), 2: 1–2.

22. Thomas Tillam, "Uppon the first sight of New-England," in *Seventeenth-Century American Poetry*, p. 397.

23. Michael Wigglesworth, op. cit.

24. Richard Steere, *Earths Felicities, Heavens Allowances*, in *Seventeenth-Century American Poetry*, p. 259.

25. John Cotton, *Gods Promise*, p. 19.

26. William Hubbard, "From Pascataqua to Pemmaquid," in *The Present State of New England*, pp. 80–81.

27. "To the Christian Reader," *The Banners of Grace and Love Displayed* (London, 1657).

28. John Cotton, *Discourse about Civil Government in a New Plantation* . . . (London, 1663), p. 35. See also Chester E. Eisinger, "The Puritans' Justification for Taking the Land," *Essex Institute Historical Collections* 84 (1948): 131–43.

29. John Winthrop, *Conclusions for the Plantation in New England* [*1629*], Old South Leaflets Series, [Boston Directors of the Old South work, 1896], 2, No. 50.

30. *Winthrop Papers*, 3: 182.

31. John Eliot, "The Conjectures," p. 14.

32. *Abstracts of the Laws of New England*. . . . (London, 1641), in Peter Force, *Tracts*, 4 vols, No. 9 (Washington, D.C., 1844), 3: 8.

33. *Winthrop Papers*, 4: 101–2.

34. Ibid., 222.

35. Ibid., 3: 182–83.

36. *The Present State of New-England*, p. 63.

37. Yi-Fu Tuan, "Attitudes Toward Environment; Themes and Approaches," in *Environmental Perception and Behavior*, ed. David Lowenthal (Chicago: Univ. of Chicago Press, 1967), p. 16.

38. Roderick Nash, *Wilderness and the American Mind* (New Haven, Conn.: Yale Univ. Press, 1967), pp. 1–22.

39. George Huntston Williams, *Wilderness and Paradise in Christian Thought* . . . (New York: Harper, 1962), p. 13.

40. Peter Carroll, *Puritanism and the Wilderness* (New York: Columbia Univ. Press, 1969).

41. George H. Williams, op. cit., p. 15.

42. John Cotton, *The Powring out of the Seven Vials* . . . (London, 1642), p. 11.

43. Henry Whitfield, "Epistle Dedicatory," *Banners of Grace and Love Displayed.*

44. Joseph Morgan, *The History of the Kingdom of Basaruah*, ed. Richard Schlatter [1715] (Cambridge, Mass.: Harvard Univ. Press, 1946).

45. John Wilson, *The Day-Breaking, If Not the Sun-Rising* . . . (London, Printed by R. Cotes, for F. Clifton, 1647), pp. 16, 23.

46. William Hubbard, *General History*, pp. 96–97.

47. Edward Johnson, *Good News from New-England*, op. cit., p. 197.

48. Benjamin Lynde, "Lines Descriptive of Thomson's Island," in *Seventeenth-Century American Poetry*, p. 493.

49. Grindall Rawson, "Upon the Death of . . . Mr. Jno Saffin Junr," in *Seventeenth-Century American Poetry*, p. 477.

50. William Bradford, "Of Boston in New England," in *Seventeenth-Century American Poetry*, p. 388–89.

51. John Higginson, *The Cause of God and His People in New-England* (Boston, 1663), pp. 10–11.

52. C. W. Chalklin, *Seventeenth-Century Kent: A Social and Economic History* (London: Longmans, 1965), p. 12.

53. Ibid.

54. William Hubbard, "Pascataqua to Pemmaquid," pp. 1–2.

55. *Winthrop Papers*, 3: 184.

56. Ibid., 4: 103–4.

57. John Eliot, "The Conjectures," p. 3.

58. C. W. Chalklin, op. cit., pp. 75, 90.

59. Cotton Mather, *The Wonders of the Invisible World* (Boston, 1693).

60. John Eliot, "The Conjectures," p. 21.

61. *Winthrop Papers*, 5: 38.

62. See Samuel Eliot Morison, *Builders of the Bay Colony* (1930; rpt. Cambridge, Mass.: Houghton Mifflin, 1964), pp. 278–79.

63. John White, op. cit., pp. 4–5.

64. John Eliot, "The Conjectures," p. 3.

65. Quoted in Oliver Ayer Roberts, *History of the . . . Ancient and Honourable Artillery Company of Massachusetts* (Boston: A. Mudge & Son, 1895), 1: 205.

THOMAS MORTON: CHARACTER AND

SYMBOL IN A MINOR AMERICAN EPIC

The interest of the belletrist in Thomas Morton, "mine Host of Ma-re-Mount," has always focused upon the May celebration which Morton sponsored on the Massachusetts coast in the spring of 1627.[1] From this clearly symbolic incident, and its consequences, have come two important literary works: Nathaniel Hawthorne's "The Maypole of Merry Mount" (1837) and much of Robert Lowell's drama, "Endecott and the Red Cross" in *The Old Glory* (1964). Lesser works, including Morton's own self-portrayal in *New English Canaan* (1637), make up the rest of Mortonia for the literary historian and aesthetician. It is a body of literature rich in false-priests, Machiavellis and anti-heroes, all tracing their lineage back to the seminal incident in which Morton confronted the Puritans at Merry Mount.

My intention here is to examine the evolution of Thomas Morton as a character and symbol in American literature, and to suggest that his role as a protean villain is related to minor epic tradition: the matter of Merry Mount. Like the matter of Troy, but on a much smaller scale, the incidents at Merry Mount were to become part of the national inherited experience, and were to be celebrated in verse, drama, song and spectacle. For three centuries Morton, as "mine Host of Ma-re-Mount," was to have an identity in aesthetic experience, at a level of reality quite different from the actual incidents recorded in history.

In 1627 Thomas Morton lived at Mt. Wollaston, a site on Massachusetts Bay only thirty miles south of the Separatist colony at Plymouth and even closer to the future site of the Puritan settlement at Salem. Morton's companions were a half-dozen adventurous men, most of whom had broken their indentures to the departed Captain Wollaston in order to become independent traders and trappers on the New England coast. When Morton erected his Maypole in 1627 he was indulging in the ancient ritual of celebrating the spring, a tradition still kept in Elizabethan England and easily traced back to the pagan practices of classical and biblical times. It was about one full year later, in June 1628, that Thomas Morton and two men were arrested by Miles Standish and a small party of soldiers. Morton was soon deported to England, and was absent from Massachusetts when John Endecott arrived with the Puritan expedition to found the colony at Salem. Endecott came south to Mt. Wollaston to cut down the Maypole, which still stood as a sea-mark to sailors and, symbolically, as a challenge to the spiritual authority of the New England theists. Morton unexpectedly returned to Plymouth in the fall of 1628, and not long after confronted Endecott at Salem in a dispute over the legality of the patents under which the Massachusetts Bay settlements were being established. Morton, a trained lawyer, a royalist, and a Church-of-England defender, was clearly an antagonist to the Puritans; he also seems to have been acting secretly on behalf of land speculators in England. Several months after this debate, Endecott tried to capture Morton at Merry Mount, but Morton escaped. In September of 1630, however, Morton was brought before a court at Charlestown and banished from New England a second time. It was following this that Endecott staged

the burning of Morton's house as the prisoner stood on the
deck of the ship returning him to England. Morton, of course,
was to return to Massachusetts again, but only after he had
written *New England Canaan*, a book whose various appeals
included anti-Puritan sentiment probably intended to influence the actions of Archbishop William Laud.[2] From the
very beginning the literary accounts of Morton's activities at
Merry Mount have a subjective, partisan quality. When later
authors collapsed the events of three years into the action of
one afternoon, and changed the nature of the participants to
create new aesthetic values, they were continuing the original
impulse towards subjectivity.

As the first *literateur* to take up the matter of Merry Mount,
Thomas Morton set a precedent which could hardly be followed. In his writing about Merry Mount it is not surprising
to find seventeenth century bibliolatry and the operations of
an eccentric Cavalier muse, as well as the satiric wit which
only a participant could bring to those new world intrigues.
Morton was amused by word-play, especially at the expense
of his enemies. To Morton, John Endecott was "a great swell-
ing fellow," "of little worth," or "Captain Littleworth." The
energetic and short Miles Standish became "Captain Shrimp
(a quondam drummer)." The mild-spoken John Winthrop
became "Joshua Temperwell" and Morton's friend, supposedly mutilated by the Puritans, "Mr. Innocence Faire-
cloth." The high point of Morton's punning is his renaming
of Mt. Wollaston, "Ma-re-Mount," a verbal feat which suggests accurately the seaside (i.e., Latin *mare*) location of the
hill on which the Maypole stood, but also forces his enemies
to associate the place with "merrie" England, which they had
risked their lives to leave. William Bradford mentions in *Of
Plymouth Plantation* that John Endecott renamed Ma-re-
Mount "Mt. Dagon" when he cut down the Maypole, thus
casting himself as the local Samson who destroyed the temple
of the Philistines, and indicating the reciprocal nature of

seventeenth-century word-play.[3] Even more striking as an indication of Morton's imagination, however, is his use of analogies to describe situations in which he found himself. Thus he paraphrases the substance of Book III, Chapter XVI of *New English Canaan* as, "How the 9 worthies put mine Host of Ma-re-Mount into the inchaunted castle at Plimmouth, and terrified him with the Monster Briareus." Later, when being returned to England, he narrates as Jonah, "in the whales belly." [4]

In "Baccanall Triumphe," 91 lines of mock-heroic verse which recreate the events surrounding his May celebration, Morton becomes the first American author to treat the matter of Merry Mount in a fully conceived literary performance (Book III, Chapter XVII).[5] Throughout this eclectic poem Morton's voice is that of the bard; his subject, the mock-epic of Merry Mount, is conceived in Homeric terms. He "sings the adventures" of "mine worthy wights" (i.e., Standish and his soldiers), "squires of low degree." Remaining detached from his own history, Morton sees himself through Separatist eyes as "Hidra," a hideous monster whose birth has been foretold by "the Magi." In this way he mocks the naive sectarians who misconstrue the *Bible* by using the inner light of personal fantasy. The Separatists are literalists of the imagination. When they contemplate the Maypole with antlers at the top and the seven Englishmen who live nearby, they see:

> . . . a hiddeous monster,
> Seaven heads it had, and twice so many feet,
> Arguing the body to be wondrous greate,
> Beside a forked taile heav'd up on high,
> As if it threaten'd battell to the skie. . . .
> (lines 10–14)

Beneath this religious fantasy Morton perceives an economic motive: the Separatists fear that Hidra will devour their "best flock," namely the profitable trade in Beaver skins. Economic

fear, not religion, is the true source of courage for the Separatists—at least to Morton.

At this point in the poem (line 49) the analogues are
changed and the sectarians, previously represented as ill-sped
Arthurian knights, biblical misinterpreters and scheming
Greeks, are presented as "Princes of Hell" intent upon removing Morton from the lower ground of Massachusetts to
the upper ground of England. They believe Morton will be
punished "above." Writing after the events, Morton knew
that the justice of the English courts had twice exonerated
him from charges levelled by Separatists and Puritans. His
poem is thus both a rhetorical attack and a self-defense;
throughout, the character of Thomas Morton is seen as falsely
understood by his enemies, and he remains superior to their
muddled schemes and accusations.

Nothing could be farther from such personal strategies of
assault and defense than Nathaniel Hawthorne's "Maypole of
Merry Mount" (1837), published exactly two centuries after
New England Canaan, and written apparently without any
direct use of Morton's text. In abstracting from "New England annalists" what he perceived as a nearly spontaneous allegory, Hawthorne bent his skill towards the depersonalization
of events at Merry Mount. The character of Thomas Morton
disappears almost entirely into a nominal figure called "Blackstone," referred to as "the Comus of the crew" and "a priest
of Baal." In *Twice-Told Tales* (1837) Hawthorne added a
footnote explaining that his character Blackstone has no relation to the Reverend William Blackstone, an early episcopal
minister in New England "not known to have been an im-
moral man." A year earlier, when the tale appeared in *The
Token* (1836), Hawthorne had named the Morton-derived
character "Claxton," and had added another ambiguous footnote disclaiming any identification between his Claxton and
the Reverend Laurence Claxton, an Anabaptist who tolerated
Maypoles but never visited New England.[6] Such scholarly

negations would seem to indicate Hawthorne's desire to avoid specific religious criticism. As an allegorist he needed abstractions: an anti-Puritan emblem, a "Black-stone" who connoted the medieval Lord of Misrule, Milton's Comus and the archetypal pagan, without pointless detail. It is largely from this maneuver on Hawthorne's part that Thomas Morton began his posthumous transformation into a figure of abstract villainy.

But Hawthorne's tale was also responsible for other changes in the literary tradition of Merry Mount. As an allegorist of the Romantic age, Hawthorne used such early nineteenth century histories as Strutt's *Book of English Sports and Pastimes* and William Hone's *Everyday Book*.[7] Both furnished him with details to create in his story the Romantic myth of a golden age. Morton and his six followers became a host of pleasure-seekers, inhabiting a grand anti-Salem, or sensual Eden, in the new world. The myth of the golden age is clearly an abstraction antithetical to the Puritan forces, and the allegory gains focus by it. In addition to this basic duality which permeates the sketch, Hawthorne found it necessary to invent new characters, collapse the original sequence of events into the confrontations of one afternoon, and shift the moral emphasis to a consideration of sexual sin. Thus we have Edward and Edith, a thinly-disguised Adam and Eve, about to be married by the false priest Blackstone in a pagan ritual. Only the timely arrival of "the Puritan of Puritans," John Endecott, saves the young lovers from a sinful union. Like the angel Michael, Endecott turns the couple out of Eden and into the world of painful realities. To achieve his meanings in one scene, Hawthorne has dismissed Miles Standish entirely and resorted to a dramatic confrontation in which Morton's paganism is defeated, and the Maypole cut down, at the height of the May revel.

Although we can appreciate the strategies of the allegorist and see his fiction as *sui generis*, unrelated to historical fact, we cannot disregard the consequences of Hawthorne's innovations in the story of Merry Mount. All later versions of the episode retain the young lovers and a message about sexual morality. In like manner Endecott thereafter replaced Miles Standish as the dramatic captor of Morton, and the complex events of three years were condensed into a sharp confrontation, usually taking place in a scene that resembled a Cecil B. DeMille film spectacle. Hawthorne's own personal themes, such as the symbolic uses of a father figure in various disguises, or his fear about matrimonial union, are part of "The Maypole of Merry Mount." Endecott is authoritative in his legislative control over the terms of a proper marriage; Hawthorne's interest in this subject thus has a resolution. For later American authors these values were part of the story of Merry Mount. In a sense, Hawthorne's emphasis upon attitudes toward sexual sin amounted to the assimilation of the material into the mainstream of American interests.

As an allegorist Hawthorne approached the matter of Merry Mount from a philosophical stance outside history. His successor, John Lothrop Motley, did just the reverse. In *Merry-Mount: a Romance of the Massachusetts Colony* (1849), the future historian tried his second and last romance before turning to history as the field which would make him famous. Motley was a close student of seventeenth-century manuscripts and had been recently trained abroad in the painstaking methodology of German historicism. On principle Motley did not read Hawthorne's tale, for he felt that, "then my own pictures would be still more unsatisfactory to me." [8] Motley did paint verbal pictures, as he knew. And he also knew, of course, that his romance was in the manner of Scott or Cooper, full of the dramatic narrative events which would hold the pictures together. Although full of accurate historic detail, Motley's view of Merry Mount is as subjective as Hawthorne's.

It is Motley's version of the May celebration which especially reveals the subjectivity of the historical romance. For

Motley the proper associations were deliberately epical, as
they had been for Thomas Morton in "Baccanall Triumphe."
Thus the Maypole is drawn to the site by fifty yoked savages,
all wearing wreathes upon their brows as they toil, and all
subjected unceasingly to a religious harangue about their im-
manent conversion from paganism to Christianity. It is not
Morton, but a lesser and more bumptious resident of Merry
Mount, who commits this particular folly. Morton himself is
seen presiding over the festivities in the garb of Robin Hood.
He has arranged epic games in which savages and Englishmen
compete for the palm of superiority in sports such as archery,
wrestling and quarterstaff. Afterwards, Morton retires to his
"palace" with his "dusky maid Marion" while other denizens
of Sherwood Forest and medieval masquers continue the revel.

The romancer, like the allegorist, works in a genre which
permits the elaborate staging of effects for emotional and intellectual reasons. Both writers are also comfortable with obvious moral judgments built into their own fictions. It is easy
to see that both authors found inspiration in the extravagant
behavior which they could extrapolate from the facts of history. And it is equally clear that Hawthorne and Motley con-
demn Morton, or his prototype, on the basis of a Puritan ethic
that is present in their fictions, both implicitly and explicitly.
What is most interesting, however, is the relish with which
they convey effects counter to the moralisms which they
would have us endorse. Their mutual fascination with pagan
lore is conveyed in literary vehicles which damn paganism in
the new world. One can conclude from this that poetic license
in the Romantic versions of Merry Mount reveals an old Puritan practice: vicarious enjoyment of the sinful.

During the age of literary realism there was an apparent
lack of interest in the matter of Merry Mount, if we look
solely to *belles lettres*.[9] But it was during this time that crucial
sources of information, such as Bradford's *Of Plymouth Plantation* and *New English Canaan* itself were made available to

the public in 1856 and 1880, respectively. The approach of
the historian to the recovered facts of Merry Mount is of particular interest from a literary point of view, for not only did
several historians reveal highly belletristic interests in the topic,
they also revealed to twentieth-century authors some of the
complexity of the subject matter. Charles Francis Adams
edited *New English Canaan* for The Prince Society in 1880
and later made Morton an important figure in his classic of
American historicism, *Three Episodes in Massachusetts History* (1892). For Adams there was no need to blend fiction
with truth. He could appreciate the symbolism of Merry
Mount objectively:

> There was a certain distance and grandeur and dignity about it,
> —a majesty of solitude, a futurity of empire. On the one hand,
> the sombre religious settlement; on the other, the noisy trading
> post, —two germs of civilized life in the immeasurable wilder-
> ness, unbroken, save at Merry-Mount and Plymouth, from the
> Penobscot to the Hudson. Yet that wilderness, though immea-
> surable to them, was not large enough for both. Merry-Mount
> was roaring out its chorus in open defiance of Plymouth, and
> Plymouth was so scandalized at the doings of Merry-Mount
> that, when he heard of them, Governor Bradford thus expressed
> himself:—
> "They allso set up a May-pole, drinking and dancing aboute
> it many days togeather, inviting Indean women, for their con-
> sorts, dancing and frisking togither, (like so many fairies, or
> furies rather,) and worse practices. As if they had anew revived
> and celebrated the feasts of the Roman Goddes Flora, or the
> beastly practieses of the madd Bachhinalains." [10]

Adams' suggestion of the "germs" of meaning, the larger
contrasts, is the approach of an objectivist. We have already
noted that John Lothrop Motley, although essentially a historian, turned to historical fiction to approach the subject.
A third extreme is possible: history which is largely fiction.
This is the nature of Henry Beston's popularized biography

of Morton in *The Gallant Vagabonds* (1925). Beston achieved
a form of creative self-expression in his treatment of Morton.
He was an open partisan of Morton's defiant stance against
the forms of religious oppression. Like Morton he perceived
economics as a stratum of truth beneath the old pieties: "Parliament had on several occasions redefined the deity and no-
body had been a penny the worse." He characterizes Morton
as a courageous cavalier in a plumed hat, long hair and Stuart
dress, a doomed "gallant" deserving of sympathy:

> What chance had this English gentleman, who knew himself to
> be a subject of King Charles and whose soul was still a subject
> of Elizabeth, in this court composed of seventeenth century
> Englishmen laboring under the extraordinary delusion that they
> were primitive Jews of the Arabian desert? [11]

In the writings of Beston we have a quasi-literary tradition, an
approach which asks for the emotional effects of literature. As
a group of historians, Motley, Adams and Beston suggest the
parameters of history as an intellectual genre: historical fiction,
history, and fictionalized history are substitutes for a realistic
treatment of the matter of Merry-Mount.

In 1937 the symbolic possibilities of Morton and Merry
Mount reached a crescendo in an opera entitled *Merry Mount:
An Opera in Four Acts and Five Scenes*. The libretto was
taken from a dramatic poem written by Richard Stokes; the
score was by the well-known composer Howard Hanson.
Richard Stokes chose to obliterate the historical Morton, just
as Hawthorne had done a century earlier. He keeps instead a
stage manager for the sinful revels, an "Abbot of Misrule"
dressed like an Anglican priest, and at one point this symbolic
character reappears in a dream as "Beelzebub, general of the
Satanic armies." This happens to be an odd reversal of Morton's symbology in "Baccanall Triumphe," where Separatists
and Puritans are figured as primary devils.

But the real significance of Stokes' use of Morton is in the displacement of the problems presented by Morton—into the psychology of another character, "Wrestling Bradford." In this unique creation Stokes has internalized the meanings of Merry Mount for a twentieth-century audience: the epic struggle between sensual pleasure and Puritan restraint is now a matter for psychological analysis. In "Wrestling Bradford" Stokes vaguely implies, by name and social position, a comparison to the revered William Bradford. But this character is a Puritan divine, like Hawthorne's Reverend Dimmsdale, and is secretly driven by lust for the non-Puritan Lady Marigold Sandys. Like Faust, he literally barters his soul to the devil for immediate worldly pleasure—possession of the lady. The Bradford character is also strangely in the position of John Endecott as destroyer of the Merry Mount establishment and Thomas Morton. Thus Wrestling Bradford is a complex of associations: Faust, Dimmsdale, Endecott, Bradford—and perhaps, Everyman. The great oppositions of sexual desire and restraint, religious piety and hypocrisy, integrity and "selling the soul" are the true themes of the opera. Against these the actual Thomas Morton, as Stokes says in his Introduction, has withdrawn into minor significance.

It is worth noting that the extravagances of popular American entertainment in the 1930s had certain similarities to the excesses of Romanticism and the creativity of the baroque. Stokes had something in common, imaginatively, with Hawthorne and Morton. Consider, for example, the epic lavishness of the stage description for the May Day scene. The following passage occurs as two flowers of English nobility, Gower and Marigold, are about to be married like Hawthorne's Edith and Edward, in a pagan ritual:

A posthorn sounds backstage and the revelers fall apart, leaving a passage. GOWER and the Worthies arise. Enter, rear center, a "coach" formed by thirty-six girls, four abreast, in compact order. Two on either side rotate white parasols, with pink ruffles, to represent wheels. MARIGOLD, borne aloft in the midst, is costumed as the goddess Flora and wears also a bridal veil with a crescent of gems at her brow. A child at the front wears a coachman's high hat with rosette and ribbons, and guides with reins of flowers two small girls who prance like ponies in the van. A second child, at the rear, is dressed as a postillion, in yellow and green, and blows a horn. GOWER descends from the throne. The "coach" advances to the front of the stage, wheels to the right and halts.[12]

The development of such fantasies in the literature of Merry Mount presents a problem for the aesthetician and historian. Clearly two things cannot be avoided: the bravura style of all opera as a genre requiring "spectacle," and the social factors of the depression years—which promoted escapist art such as the dance extravaganzas of Busby Berkley. But in particular Stokes, like Robert Lowell after him, saw the meaning of Merry Mount in terms of the personal struggle of a major character. In this sense the physical display with which the meaning of Merry Mount is developed is less important than the emphasis upon psychological problems.

The difficulty of understanding the truth about Morton, at least in recent years, is summed up by a character in H. L. Davidson's novel *The Disturber* (1964): "I'd be damned if I understood his nonsense, try as I would. It sounded brave but it made no sense." [13] In this novel about the Merry Mount episode the author popularizes the subject, and uses naturalistic dialogue uneasily to do it. The result is an undistinguished addition to the literature of Merry Mount, at least in contrast to Robert Lowell's "Endecott and the Red Cross," which appeared in the same year, 1964.

Robert Lowell's portrait of Morton is the most intellectually stimulating in American literature. For the first time Morton is both restored to his historic role and redeemed from the past as a character worthy of our close inspection. Lowell clarifies in his play the connections between English and colonial politics—although his pro-revolutionary thesis simplifies the finer details of the actual intriguing. Likewise he retains Morton's association with the English church through an affiliation with an Episcopal minister named "Blackstone." Lowell's updating of the old conflicts can be traced to his thorough commitment to liberal and radical causes in contemporary American politics. His version of Morton reveals an exploiter of redmen, a self-seeking entrepreneur, an "establishment" agent, and, oddly enough, a false Christ.

In the short introductory scene which introduces the play the setting is a nether-world of symbolic elements; in this place the Morton character has a special ambience. He is entirely disconnected from his own dialogue later as a manipulator who will be squelched by John Endecott.[14] In the symbol-world Morton receives an Indian Sachem as "brother and father," and trades guns and powder for furs. The Sachem has been falsely informed in a dream that Morton alone is the white man whom he can trust, and so the Indian gives to Morton his daughter. For Lowell, economic exploitation is followed by sexual exploitation—or so I interpret the gesture. In addition, the materials have a racist implication, and Morton appears to be a symbol of America's first racist. As if this is not enough, later in the play Morton clearly represents the concealed interests of England in its exploitation of the colonists. He is the devious establishment enemy. In all these ways Thomas Morton represents a contemporary villainy against which true Americans will rebel. And, of course, the message of the play is that the true "old glory" of America is its revolutionary ardor, the fact that it does rebel against the manifold iniquities of men like Thomas Morton.

Like Richard Stokes, Lowell focuses in one character the essential conflicts of the Merry Mount drama. Lowell's John Endecott is a mellowed political activist, a man whose once-hard doctrines have been softened by experience and human sympathy. He is inclined to let Morton, and Blackstone, and the two young lovers, and the offending Indians, go relatively free, with minor punishment. But he realizes in time that such leniency is moral backsliding. If he does not punish the captured revelers severely, and defy English authority with colonial power, the result will be the eventual victimization of America by men with old world mentalities like Morton's. For Endecott the true act then becomes harsh punishment of Morton and symbolic mutilation of the British flag. This is *The Old Glory*, the title and the message, of Lowell's dramatic trilogy.

The emergence of Thomas Morton onto the stages of the twentieth century suggests the natural gravitation of a symbol to an appropriate literary mode. In the public auditorium the meaning of Morton of Merry Mount can be considered by the masses. The meanings suggested by "mine Host" now have a contemporary significance, having to do with the moral nature of America and the choices of individual men. We might even say that in our time the problem of viewing the symbolic incidents at Mt. Wollaston have become an inherent part of their meaning. Thus, although the Puritans continue to conquer in American literature just as they did in history, the dilemma presented by confronting pagan freedom with Puritan self-control remains unresolved—it is part of the American tradition of defining the American character. The potential meaning of the matter of Merry Mount is thus inextricable from the search for a nascent and independent American identity.

ROBERT J. GANGEWERE
CARNEGIE-MELLON UNIVERSITY

Notes

1. The exact date of the erection of the Maypole is discussed in Donald Francis Connors, *Thomas Morton* (New York: Twayne, 1969), p. 151, and in Charles Francis Adams, Jr., ed., *The New English Canaan of Thomas*

Morton (Boston, 1883), pp. 17–18. Neither Morton nor his contemporaries are precise about the date.

2. Connors, pp. 24–25.

3. William Bradford, *History of Plymouth Plantation, 1620–1647*, ed. William T. Davis (New York: Scribner's, 1908, 1920), p. 238.

4. References to *New English Canaan* . . . are from the original text on microfilm; Thomas Morton, *New English Canaan or New Canaan . .* (Amsterdam: J. F. Stam, 1637). (Microfilm Series: "Books Printed in England Before 1640," No. 967.)

5. I follow here the usage of Connors in titling the poem, "Baccanall Triumphe." Morton actually titles the verse, "THE POEM," and leads up to it by saying it is of the type known as a Baccanall Triumphe. See *New English Canaan*, pp. 145–46.

6. *The Complete Works of Nathaniel Hawthorne*, vol. 1: *Twice Told Tales* (Boston and New York: Houghton, Mifflin, 1888), 77.

7. Daniel G. Hoffman argues this persuasively in *Form and Fable in American Fiction* (New York: Oxford Univ. Press, 1961), p. 144.

8. [John Lothrop Motley], *Merry Mount: A Romance of the Massachusetts Colony* (Boston: J. Munroe and Co., 1849), 1: 5.

9. Connors, p. 123 ff.

10. Charles Francis Adams, *Three Episodes of Massachusetts History* . . . (New York: Houghton, Mifflin, 1892), 1: 182.

11. Henry Beston [Sheahan], *The Book of Gallant Vagabonds* (New York: George H. Doran Co., 1925), p. 166.

12. Richard Leroy Stokes, *Merry Mount: A Dramatic Poem for Music in Three Acts of Six Scenes* (New York: Farrar & Rinehart, 1937), p. 62.

13. Quoted in Connors, p. 127.

14. Robert Lowell, *The Old Glory* (New York: Farrar, Straus & Giroux, 1964), pp. 5–8.

NOTES ON THE CONTRIBUTORS

Robert D. Arner is Professor of English at the University of Cincinnati and a member of the Executive Committee of the Early American Literature Group of the MLA. He is the author of numerous articles and notes which have appeared in *Early American Literature, The Southern Literary Journal, New England Quarterly, Tennessee Studies in Literature, Criticism,* and elsewhere and is currently at work on books on Samuel Sewall and Comic Literature in Colonial America.

Thomas M. Davis, Professor of English at Kent State University, is the author of several articles on Edward Taylor, including Taylor's unpublished poetry and prose. He is currently working on an edition of Taylor's works.

Arthur Forstater is a doctoral candidate in Medieval Studies at Kent State University. His minor area of interest is American Puritanism.

Robert Jay Gangewere is Editor of *Carnegie Magazine,* the publication of Carnegie Institute, Pittsburgh, Pennsylvania. After receiving the Ph.D. in English from the University of Connecticut in 1966, he taught American literature at several universities in this country and abroad. His dissertation was on "The Aesthetic Theory of Wallace Stevens." He is the editor of *The Exploited Eden: Literature on the American Environment* (Harper and Row, 1972), an anthology of environmentalist writings from

Colonial times to the present. He is currently at work upon a co-authored study, *The Long Verdict, 1906–1951: Interpretations of the Crime Called an American Tragedy.*

Julian Mates is Professor of English and Dean of the School of the Arts of the C. W. Post Center of Long Island University. He is author of *The American Musical Stage Before 1800* and (with Eugene B. Cantelupe) *Renaissance Culture: A New Sense of Order,* in addition to numerous articles and reviews on the American theatre.

Harrison T. Meserole is Professor of English and Director of the Center for Bibliography at The Pennsylvania State University, and since 1966 has been the Bibliographer of the Modern Language Association and editor-in-chief of the *MLA International Bibliography.* Author of *Seventeenth-Century American Poetry* (1968) and *American Literature: Tradition and Innovation* (1969), he has contributed essays to numerous scholarly journals and to *Essays on Shakespeare* (1965), *Shakespeare 1971* (1972), and *Directions in Literary Criticism* (1973). Editor of *Seventeenth-Century News,* he is now preparing an edition of David Dunster's *Gospelmanna* and, with Harold Jantz, is editing *The Bee Hive* by Francis Daniel Pastorius.

Roger B. Stein, Associate Professor of English at the State University of New York at Binghamton and author of *John Ruskin and Aesthetic Thought in America, 1840–1900* and *The View and the Vision: Landscape Painting in 19th-Century America,* is at work on several studies of the interrelation of the arts in America, including a book on literary and visual seascape of which the present essay is a part. He is also responsible for the 1975 exhibition of *Seascape and the American Imagination* at the Whitney Museum of American Art.

Cecelia Tichi has divided a dozen articles between colonial and nineteenth-century America on such figures as Charles Brockden Brown, Longfellow, and Melville, appearing in *AL, W&MQ, EAL, Genre,* and *ELH.* She is at work on a lengthy study of Americans' impulse to reform their environment from the Puritan era through the mid-nineteenth century. She teaches on the English staff at Boston University.

INDEX